C++ Programs to Accompany Programming Logic and Design

Jo Ann Smith

COURSE TECHNOLOGY
CENGAGE Learning™

Australia • Brazil • Japan • Korea • Mexico • Singapore • Spain • United Kingdom • United States

COURSE TECHNOLOGY
CENGAGE Learning™

C++ Programs to Accompany Programming Logic and Design
Jo Ann Smith

Executive Editor: Marie Lee

Acquisitions Editor: Amy Jollymore

Managing Editor: Tricia Coia

Developmental Editor: Ann Shaffer

Editorial Assistant: Julia Leroux-Lindsey

Marketing Manager: Bryant Chrzan

Content Project Manager:
Matt Hutchinson

Art Director: Marissa Falco

Manufacturing Coordinator:
Julio Esperas

Proofreader: Suzanne Huizenga

Compositor: International Typesetting
and Composition

For product information and technology assistance, contact us at
Cengage Learning Customer & Sales Support, 1-800-354-9706

For permission to use material from this text or product,
submit all requests online at **www.cengage.com/permissions**
Further permissions questions can be e-mailed to
permissionrequest@cengage.com

ISBN-13: 978-0-324-78144-1

ISBN-10: 0-324-78144-X

Course Technology
20 Channel Center Street
Boston, MA 02210
USA

Cengage Learning is a leading provider of customized learning solutions with office locations around the globe, including Singapore, the United Kingdom, Australia, Mexico, Brazil, and Japan. Locate your local office at: **www.international.cengage.com/region**

Cengage Learning products are represented in Canada by Nelson Education, Ltd.

To learn more about Course Technology, visit
www.cengage.com/coursetechnology

To learn more about Cengage Learning, visit **www.cengage.com**

Purchase any of our products at your local college store or at our preferred online store **www.ichapters.com**

Printed in Canada
1 2 3 4 5 6 7 14 13 12 11 10

BRIEF CONTENTS

CONTENTS

CONTENTS

CONTENTS

CONTENTS

CONTENTS

PREFACE

C++ Programs to Accompany Programming Logic and Design (also known as ***C++ PAL***) is designed to provide students with an opportunity to write C++ programs as part of an Introductory Programming Logic course. It is written to be a companion text to the student's primary text, *Programming Logic and Design, Fifth Edition*, by Joyce Farrell. This textbook assumes no programming language experience and provides the beginning programmer with a guide to writing structured programs and simple object-oriented programs using introductory elements of the popular C++ programming language. It is not intended to be a textbook for a course in C++ programming. The writing is non-technical and emphasizes good programming practices. The examples do not assume mathematical background beyond high school math. Additionally, the examples illustrate one or two major points; they do not contain so many features that students become lost following irrelevant and extraneous details.

The examples in C++ PAL are often examples presented in the primary textbook, *Programming Logic and Design, Fifth Edition*. The following table shows the correlation between topics in the two books.

C++PAL	Programming Logic and Design, Fifth Edition
Chapter 1: An Introduction to C++ and the C++ Programming Environment	Chapter 1: An Overview of Computers and Logic
Chapter 2: Variables, Operators, and Writing Programs Using Sequential Statements	Chapter 1: An Overview of Computers and Logic
Chapter 3: Writing Structured C++ Programs	Chapter 2: Understanding Structure Chapter 3: The Program Planning Process: Documentation and Design
Chapter 4: Writing Programs that Make Decisions	Chapter 4: Making Decisions
Chapter 5: Writing Programs Using Loops	Chapter 5: Looping
Chapter 6: Using Arrays in C++ Programs	Chapter 6: Arrays
Chapter 7: Using Functions in C++ Programs	Chapter 7: Using Methods
Chapter 8: Writing Control Break Programs in C++	Chapter 8: Control Breaks
Chapter 9: Sorting Data and File Input/Output	Chapter 9: Advanced Array Manipulation Chapter 10: File Handling and Applications (Comprehensive edition only)
Chapter 10: Object Oriented C++	Chapter 11: Object-oriented Programming (Comprehensive edition only)

ORGANIZATION AND COVERAGE

C++ PAL provides students with a review of the programming concepts they are introduced to in their primary textbook. It also shows them how to use C++ to transform their program logic and design into working programs. The structure of a C++ program, how to compile and run a C++ console program, and introductory object-oriented concepts are introduced in Chapter 1. Chapter 2 discusses C++'s data types, variables, arithmetic and assignment operators, and using sequential statements to write a complete C++ program. In Chapter 3, students learn how to transform pseudocode and flowcharts into C++ programs. Chapters 4 and 5 introduce students to writing C++ programs that make decisions and programs that use looping constructs. Students learn to use C++ to develop more sophisticated programs that include using arrays and passing parameters to functions in Chapters 6 and 7. In Chapter 8, students learn to write control break programs. Sorting data items in an array and file input and output is introduced in Chapter 9. Lastly, in Chapter 10, students learn about writing C++ programs that include programmer-defined classes.

This book combines text explanation of concepts and syntax along with pseudocode and actual C++ code examples to provide students with the knowledge they need to implement their logic and program designs using the C++ programming language. This book is written in a modular format and provides paper and pencil exercises as well as lab exercises after each major topic is introduced. The exercises provide students with experience in reading and writing C++ code as well as modifying and debugging existing code. In the labs, students are asked to complete partially pre-written C++ programs. Using partially pre-written programs allows students to focus on individual concepts rather than an entire program. The labs also allow students the opportunity to see their programs execute.

C++ PAL is unique because:

» It is written and designed to correspond to the topics in the primary textbook, *Programming Language and Design, Fifth Edition.*

» The examples are everyday examples; no special knowledge of mathematics, accounting, or other disciplines is assumed.

» It introduces students to introductory elements of the C++ programming language rather than overwhelming beginning programmers with more detail than they are prepared to use or understand.

» Text explanations are interspersed with pseudocode from the primary book, thus reinforcing the importance of programming logic.

» Complex programs are built through the use of complete examples. Students see how an application is built from start to finish instead of studying only segments of programs.

FEATURES OF THE TEXT

Every chapter in this book includes the following features. These features are both conducive to learning in the classroom and enable students to learn the material at their own pace.

» Objectives: Each chapter begins with a list of objectives so the student knows the topics that will be presented in the chapter. In addition to providing a quick reference to topics covered, this feature provides a useful study aid.

» Figures and illustrations: This book has plenty of visuals, which provide the reader with a more complete learning experience, rather than one that involves simply studying text.

» Notes: These notes provide additional information—for example, a common error to watch out for.

» NOTE

» Exercises: Each section of each chapter includes meaningful paper and pencil exercises that allow students to practice the skills and concepts they are learning in the section.

» Labs: Each section of each chapter includes meaningful lab work that allows students to write and execute programs that implement their logic and program design.

ACKNOWLEDGMENTS

I would like to thank all of the people who helped to make this book possible, especially Ann Shaffer, Developmental Editor, whose expertise and attention to detail have made this a better textbook. She also provided encouragement, patience, humor, and flexibility when needed. Thanks also to Tricia Coia, Managing Editor, for her help and encouragement. It is a pleasure to work with these fine people who are dedicated to producing quality instructional materials.

I am grateful to the many reviewers who provided helpful and insightful comments during the development of this book, including Matthew Alimagham, Spartanburg Community College; Ruth Tucker Bogart, University of Phoenix – Online; Fred D'Angelo, Pima Community College; and Robert Dollinger, University of Wisconsin – Stevens Point.

I am dedicating this book to all of the teachers I have had the honor to know.

Jo Ann Smith

READ THIS BEFORE YOU BEGIN

TO THE USER

DATA FILES

To complete most of the lab exercises, you will need data files that have been created for this book. Your instructor will provide the data files to you. You also can obtain the files electronically from the Course Technology Web site by connecting to *www.course.com*, and then searching for this book title.

You can use a computer in your school lab or your own computer to complete the lab exercises in this book.

SOLUTIONS

Solutions to the Exercises and Labs are provided to instructors on the Course Technology Web site at *www.course.com*. The solutions are password protected.

USING YOUR OWN COMPUTER

To use your own computer to complete the material in this textbook, you will need the following:

» Computer with a 1.6 GHz or faster processor
» Operating System:
  » Windows Vista® (x86 & x64) - all editions except Starter Edition
  » Windows® XP (x86 & x64) with Service Pack 2 or later - all editions except Starter Edition
  » Windows Server® 2003 (x86 & x64) with Service Pack 1 or later (all editions)
  » Windows Server 2003 R2 (x86 and x64) or later (all editions)
» 384 MB of RAM or more (768 MB of RAM or more for Windows Vista)
» 2.2 GB of available hard-disk space
» 5400 RPM hard drive
» 1024 x 768 or higher-resolution display
» DVD-ROM Drive Is

This book was written using Microsoft Windows Vista and Quality Assurance tested using Microsoft Windows Vista.

UPDATING YOUR PATH ENVIRONMENT VARIABLE

» Setting the PATH variable allows you to use the compiler (c1) and execute your programs without having to specify the full path for the command.

» To set the PATH permanently in Windows XP and Vista:

1. Open the Control Panel, and then double click **System**.

2. In Windows XP, select the **Advanced** Tab and then click the **Environment Variables** button. In Windows Vista, click the **Advanced system settings** link, click **Continue** in the User Account Control window, and then click the **Environment Variables** button.

3. Look for "PATH" or "Path" in the User variables or System variables area. Select **PATH** or **Path**, click **Edit**, and then edit the PATH variable by adding ;C:\Program Files\Microsoft Visual Studio 9.0\vc\bin. If you are not sure where to add the path, add it to the right end of the "PATH". A typical PATH might look like this C:\Windows;C:\Windows\Command;C:\Program Files\Microsoft Visual Studio 9.0.\vc\bin.

» Capitalization does not matter when you are setting the PATH variable. The PATH is a series of folders separated by semi-colons (;). Windows searches for programs in the PATH folders in order, from left to right.

» To find out the current value of your PATH, open a Command Prompt window, type: **path** and then press **Enter**

» Once your PATH is set, you must execute the following command in a Command Prompt window to set the environment variables for the Visual C++ compiler: type **vcvars32** and then press **Enter**

TO THE INSTRUCTOR

To complete some of the Exercises and Labs in this book, your students must use the data files provided with this book. These files are available on the Course Technology Web site at *www.course.com*. Follow the instructions in the Help file to copy the data files to your server or standalone computer. You can view the Help file using a text editor such as WordPad or Notepad. Once the files are copied, you may instruct your students to copy the files to their own computers or workstations.

COURSE TECHNOLOGY DATA FILES

You are granted a license to copy the data files to any computer or computer network used by individuals who have purchased this book.

1

AN INTRODUCTION TO C++ AND THE C++ PROGRAMMING ENVIRONMENT

After studying this chapter, you will be able to:

Discuss the C++ programming language and its history

Explain introductory concepts and terminology used in object-oriented programming

Recognize the structure of a C++ program

Complete the C++ development cycle, which includes creating a source code file, compiling the source code, and executing a C++ program

You should do the exercises and labs in this chapter only after you have finished Chapter 1 of your book, *Programming Logic and Design, Fifth Edition*, by Joyce Farrell. This chapter introduces the C++ programming language and its history. It explains some introductory object-oriented concepts, and describes the process of compiling and executing a C++ program. You begin writing C++ programs in Chapter 2 of this book.

THE C++ PROGRAMMING LANGUAGE

The C programming language was written in the early 1970s by Dennis Ritchie at AT&T Bell Labs. C is an important programming language because it is both a high level and a low level programming language. It is a **high level language**, which means that it is more English-like and easier for programmers to use than a low level language. At the same time, it possesses **low level language** capabilities that allow programmers to directly manipulate the underlying computer hardware.

▶▶ NOTE
Due to their power, C and C++ have been used in the programming of special effects for action movies and video games.

The C++ programming language was developed by Bjarne Stroustrup at AT&T Bell Labs in 1979 and inherited the wide-spread popularity of C. Because many programmers liked using the powerful C programming language, it was an easy step to move on to the new C++ language.

What makes C++ especially useful for today's programmers is that it is an object-oriented programming language. The term **object-oriented** encompasses a number of concepts explained later in this chapter and throughout this book. For now, all you need to know is that an object-oriented programming language is modular in nature, allowing the programmer to build a program from reusable parts of programs called classes.

AN INTRODUCTION TO OBJECT-ORIENTED TERMINOLOGY

You must understand a few object-oriented concepts to be successful at reading and working with C++ programs in this book. Note, however, that you will not learn enough to make you a C++ programmer. You will have to take additional courses in C++ to become a C++ programmer. This book teaches you only the basics.

To fully understand the term "object-oriented," you need to know a little about procedural programming. Procedural programming is a style of programming that is older than object-oriented programming. Procedural programs consist of statements that the computer runs or **executes**. Many of the statements make calls (a request to run or execute) to groups of other statements that are known as procedures, modules, methods, or subroutines. Therefore, these programs are known as "procedural" because they perform a sequence of procedures. Procedural programming focuses on writing code that takes some data (for example, some sales figures), performs a specific task using the data (for example, adding up the sales figures), and then produces output (for example, a sales report). When people who use procedural programs (the **users**) decide that they want their programs to do something slightly different, a programmer revises the program code, taking great care not to introduce errors into the logic of the program.

Today, we need computer programs that are more flexible and easier to revise. Object-oriented programming languages, including C++, were introduced to meet this need. In object-oriented programming, the programmer can focus on the data that he or she wants to manipulate, rather than the individual lines of code required to manipulate that data (although those individual lines still must be written eventually). An object-oriented program is made up of a collection of interacting objects. An **object** represents something in the real world, such as a car, an employee, a video game character, or an item in an inventory. An object includes (or **encapsulates**) both the data related to the object and the tasks you can perform on that data. The term **behavior** is sometimes used to refer to the tasks you can perform on an object's data. For example, the data for an inventory object might include a list of inventory items, the number of each item in stock, the number of days each item has been in stock, and so on. The behaviors of the inventory object might include calculations that add up the total number of items in stock and calculations that determine the average amount of time each item remains in inventory.

In object-oriented programming, the data items within an object are known collectively as the object's **attributes**. You can think of an attribute as one of the characteristics of an object, such as its shape, its color, or its name. The tasks the object performs on that data are known as the object's **methods**. (You can also think of a method as an object's behavior.) Because methods are built into objects, when you create a C++ program, you don't always have to write line after line of code telling the program exactly how to manipulate the object's data. Instead, you can write a shorter line of code, known as a **call**, that passes a message to the method indicating that you need it to do something.

» NOTE
The preceding assumes you are using classes that someone else previously developed. That programmer must write code that manipulates the object's data.

For example, you can display dialog boxes, scroll bars, and buttons for a user of your program to type in or click on simply by sending a message to an existing object because programmers at Microsoft included these classes that you can use. At other times, you will be responsible for creating your own classes and writing the code for the methods that are part of that class. Whether you use existing, prewritten classes or create your own classes, one of your main jobs as a C++ programmer is to communicate with the various objects in a program (and the methods of those objects) by passing messages. Individual objects in a program can also pass messages to other objects.

When programmers write an object-oriented program, they begin by creating a class. A **class** can be thought of as a template for a group of similar objects. In a class, the programmer specifies the data (attributes) and behaviors (methods) for all objects that belong to that class. An object is sometimes referred to as an **instance** of a class, and the process of creating an object is referred to as **instantiation**.

To understand the terms "class," "instance," and "instantiation," it's helpful to think of them in terms of a real-world example—baking a chocolate cake. The recipe is similar to a class and an actual cake is an object. If you wanted to, you could create many chocolate cakes that are all based on the same recipe. For example, your mother's birthday cake, your sister's anniversary cake, and the cake for your neighborhood bake sale all might be based on a single recipe that contains the same data (ingredients) and methods (instructions). In object-oriented programming, you can create as many objects as you need in your program from the same class.

THE STRUCTURE OF A C++ PROGRAM

When a programmer learns a new programming language, the first program he or she traditionally writes is a Hello World program—a program that displays the message "Hello World" on the screen. Creating this simple program illustrates that the language is capable of instructing the computer to communicate with the "outside" world. The C++ version of the Hello World program is shown in Figure 1-1:

```
#include <iostream>
using namespace std;
int main()
{
    cout << "Hello World" << endl;
    return 0;
}
```

Figure 1-1 Hello World program

At this point, you're not expected to understand all the code in Figure 1-1. Just notice that the code begins with the preprocessor directive, `#include <iostream>`. The C++ **preprocessor** is a program that processes your C++ program before the compiler processes it. The `#include` directive tells the compiler to include another file when the program is compiled. This makes it easy for you to use code previously written by you or others in your programs without having to recreate it. You will learn more about the Visual C++ compiler later in this chapter. Following the `#include` you see `<iostream>`, which is the name of a header file you want to include in this program. The **iostream header file** gives your program access to what it needs to perform input and output in a C++ program. The name of the header file is placed within angle brackets (< >). The angle brackets tell the compiler to look for this file in a directory that is specified by the compiler you are using. You will learn more about preprocessor directives throughout this book.

> **▶▶ NOTE**
> Namespaces are a relatively new addition to C++ and are used primarily in large programs. In this book, the only namespace you will use is the `std` namespace.

The next line (`using namespace std;`) instructs the compiler to use the `std` namespace. You can think of a **namespace** as a container that holds various program elements. The **std** namespace contains everything C++ programs need to use the Standard C++ library. The **Standard C++ library** adds functionality to the C++ programming language. For example, this program needs to use the `std` namespace to have access to `cout` and `endl`, which you see on the fifth line in Figure 1-1. Notice that this line ends with a semicolon (;). In fact, all C++ statements end with a semicolon. The reason the previous line, `#include <iostream>`, does not end with a semicolon is that it is a preprocessor directive, not a C++ statement.

> **▶▶ NOTE**
> You can tell `main` is a function because of the parentheses; all C++ function names are followed by parentheses.

On the third line you see the start of a function named `main`. A **function** is a group of C++ statements that perform a specified task. This is a special function in a C++ program; the `main` function is the first function that executes when any program runs. The programs in the first six chapters of this book will include only a main function. In later chapters you will be able to include additional functions.

The first part of any function is its **header**. In Figure 1-1, the header for the main function begins with the int keyword, followed by the function name, which is main. A **keyword** is a special word that is reserved by C++ to have a special meaning. To understand the keyword int you need to know that functions often send values back to a calling function (for example, the result of a calculation), which can then be used elsewhere in the program. Another way to say this is that functions sometimes return a value. In Figure 1-1, the keyword int indicates that the main function returns an integer. You will learn more about functions returning values in Chapter 7 of this book.

The opening curly brace ({) on the fourth line of Figure 1-1 marks the beginning of the body of the main function and the closing curly brace (}) on the last line of Figure 1-1 marks the end of the main function. All the code within this pair of curly braces executes when the main function executes. In Figure 1-1, there are two lines of code between the curly braces. The first is:

```
cout << "Hello World" << endl;
```

This is the line that causes the words Hello World to appear on the user's screen. This line consists of multiple parts. The first part, cout, is the name of an object that represents the user's screen. Next, you see << which is called the **insertion** or **output** operator. You use cout and << to output what follows, which in this example is the string constant "Hello World". (The quotation marks will not appear on the screen, but they are necessary to make the program work.) After "Hello World" you see another << which causes endl to be displayed (after Hello World) on the user's screen. For now, think of endl as a **newline** that causes the cursor to be positioned on the line after Hello World. You will learn more about endl in Chapter 9 of this book. Note that the semicolon that ends the cout << "Hello World" << endl; statement is required because it tells the compiler that this is the end of the statement.

> **▶▶NOTE**
> Don't confuse the last character in endl, '1' (el), with the digit '1' (one).

The next line of code is return 0;. This statement instructs the compiler to return the value 0 from the main function. Remember, when you saw the header for the main function on the third line of this program, you used the keyword int to specify that the main function returns an integer; 0 is the returned integer. Conventionally, when a program returns a 0, it means "everything went well and the program is finished."

Next, you learn about the C++ development cycle so that later in this chapter, you can compile the Hello World program and execute it.

THE C++ DEVELOPMENT CYCLE

When you finish designing a program and writing the C++ code that implements your design, you must compile and execute your program. This three-step process of writing code, compiling code, and executing code is called the C++ development cycle. It is illustrated in Figure 1-2.

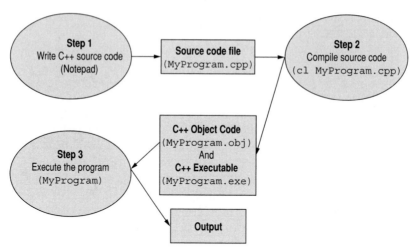

Figure 1-2 The C++ development cycle

Let's begin by learning about Step 1, writing the C++ source code.

WRITING C++ SOURCE CODE

As you learned in the previous section, you write a C++ program by creating a function named main that contains C++ statements. But what do you use to write the program, and where do you save it?

One method you can use to write a C++ program is to use a text editor, such as the Windows text editor, Notepad. You can use any text editor, but the steps in this book assume you are using Notepad. To start Notepad, click the Start button, select Programs or All Programs, select Accessories, and then select Notepad. Once Notepad starts, you simply type in your C++ source code. **Source code** is the name used for the statements that make up a C++ program. For example, the code shown earlier in Figure 1-1 is source code.

When you save the file that contains the source code, it is important to give the file a meaningful name, and then add the extension .cpp. For the Hello World program, an appropriate name for the source code file is HelloWorld.cpp. Of course, it is also important to remember the location of the folder in which you choose to save your source code file.

You move on to Step 2 of the C++ development cycle after saving your source code file. In Step 2, you compile the source code.

COMPILING A C++ PROGRAM

The Visual C++ compiler is named **cl**. It is a program that is responsible for a two-step process that takes your source code and transforms it into object code and then links the object code to create executable code.

Object code is code in computer-readable form that is linked with libraries to create an executable file. **Executable code** is the 1s and 0s that a computer needs to execute a program.

The C++ compiler automatically saves the object code in a file. This file has the same name as the source code file, but it has an `.obj` extension rather than a `.cpp` extension.

The following steps show how to compile a source code file. These steps assume you have already created and saved the `HelloWorld.cpp` source code file.

1. Set your `PATH` environment variable. Refer to "Read This Before You Begin" at the beginning of this book for instructions on how to set the `PATH` environment variable.

> **»NOTE** If you are working in a school computer lab, these steps might already have been performed for you. If you do not know how to set the `PATH`, refer to the "Read This Before You Begin" section at the beginning of this book or ask your instructor for further information.

> **»NOTE**
> The `PATH` environment variable tells your operating system which directories on your system contain commands.

2. Open a Command Prompt window. To do this in Windows XP, click the Start button, select All Programs, select Accessories, and then select Command Prompt. In Vista, click the Start button, select All Programs, select Accessories, and then select Command Prompt. The cursor blinks to the right of the current file path. To compile your source code file, you first have to change to the file path containing your source code file. To do this, type **cd driveletter:\path** where **driveletter** is the drive containing your file, and **path** is the path to the folder containing your file. For example, to gain access to a file stored in a folder named Testing, which is in turn stored in a folder named My Program, which is stored on the c: drive, you would type **cd c:\My Program\Testing**. After you type the command, press Enter. The cursor now blinks next to the file path for the folder containing your source code file.

3. Type the following command, which uses the C++ compiler , `cl`, to compile the program:

```
cl HelloWorld.cpp
```

If there are no syntax errors in your source code, a file named `HelloWorld.obj` and a file named `HelloWorld.exe` are created. You do not see anything special happen. However, the files you just created contain the object code (`HelloWorld.obj`) and executable code (`HelloWorld.exe`) for the Hello World program. If there are syntax errors, you will see error messages on the screen; in that case, you need to go back to Notepad to fix the errors, save the source code file again, and recompile until there are no syntax errors remaining. **Syntax errors** are messages from the compiler that tell you what your errors are and where they are located in your source code file. For example, omitting a semicolon at the end of the statement `cout << "Hello World" << endl` results in a syntax error.

4. After the program is compiled, you can use the `dir` command to display a directory listing to see the files named `HelloWorld.obj` and `HelloWorld.exe`. To execute the `dir` command, you type **dir** at the command prompt. For example, if your source code file is located at **c:\My Program\Testing**, the command prompt and `dir` command should look like this: c:\My Program\Testing> dir. The `HelloWorld.obj` and `HelloWorld.exe` files should be in the same directory as the source code file `HelloWorld.cpp`.

> **»NOTE**
> At this point in your programming career, don't expect to understand the contents of files with an `.obj` or `.exe` extension if you open one using a text editor such as Notepad.

Step 3 in the development cycle is executing the C++ program. You'll learn about that next.

EXECUTING A C++ PROGRAM

To execute the Hello World program, do the following:

1. Open a Command Prompt window. To do this in Windows XP, click the Start button, select All Programs, select Accessories, and then select Command Prompt. In Vista, click the Start button, select All Programs, select Accessories, and then select Command Prompt. Change to the file path containing your executable code file, if necessary, and then enter the following command:

   ```
   HelloWorld
   ```

2. When the program executes, the words Hello World appear in the Command Prompt window.

Figure 1-3 illustrates the steps involved in compiling HelloWorld.cpp using the cl compiler, executing the dir command to verify that the files HelloWorld.obj and HelloWorld.exe were created, and the output generated by executing the Hello World program.

```
C:\Users\Jo Ann\C++ Pal\Chapter_1\Student>cl HelloWorld.cpp
Microsoft (R) 32-bit C/C++ Optimizing Compiler Version 15.00.21022.08 for 80x86
Copyright (C) Microsoft Corporation.  All rights reserved.

HelloWorld.cpp
C:\Program Files\Microsoft Visual Studio 9.0\VC\INCLUDE\xlocale(342) : warning
4530: C++ exception handler used, but unwind semantics are not enabled. Specify
/EHsc
Microsoft (R) Incremental Linker Version 9.00.21022.08
Copyright (C) Microsoft Corporation.  All rights reserved.

/out:HelloWorld.exe
HelloWorld.obj

C:\Users\Jo Ann\C++ Pal\Chapter_1\Student>dir
 Volume in drive C is OS
 Volume Serial Number is BC42-7996

 Directory of C:\Users\Jo Ann\C++ Pal\Chapter_1\Student

05/01/2008  10:23 AM    <DIR>          .
05/01/2008  10:23 AM    <DIR>          ..
05/01/2008  10:16 AM                104 HelloWorld.cpp
05/05/2008  09:16 AM             97,792 HelloWorld.exe
05/05/2008  09:16 AM             37,595 HelloWorld.obj
               3 File(s)        135,491 bytes
               2 Dir(s)  71,971,971,072 bytes free
C:\Users\Jo Ann\C++ Pal\Chapter_1\Student>HelloWorld
Hello World

C:\Users\Jo Ann\C++ Pal\Chapter_1\Student>
```

Figure 1-3 Compiling and executing the Hello World program

EXERCISE 1-1: UNDERSTANDING THE C++ COMPILER

In this exercise, assume you have written a C++ program and stored your source code in a file named FirstCPlusPlusProgram.cpp. Answer the following questions:

1. What command would you use to compile the source code?

   _____

2. What command would you use to execute the program?

   _____

LAB 1.1: COMPILING AND EXECUTING A C++ PROGRAM

In this lab, you compile and execute a prewritten C++ program, and then answer some questions about the program.

1. Open the source code file named GoodDay.cpp using Notepad or the text editor of your choice.

2. Save this source code file in a directory of your choice, and then change to that directory.

3. Compile the source code file. There should be no syntax errors. Record the command you used to compile the source code file.

   _____

   _____

4. Execute the program. Record the command you used to execute the program and also record the output of this program.

   _____

   _____

5. Modify the program so that it displays Congratulations. Save the file as Congratulations.cpp. Compile and execute.

6. Modify the Congratulations program so that it prints two lines of output. Add a second output statement that displays "Have a great day." Save the modified file as Congratulations2.cpp. Compile and execute the program.

2

VARIABLES, OPERATORS, AND WRITING PROGRAMS USING SEQUENTIAL STATEMENTS

After studying this chapter, you will be able to:

Name variables and use appropriate data types

Declare and initialize variables

Use arithmetic operators in expressions

Use assignment operators in assignment statements

Write programs using sequential statements and
interactive input statements

In this chapter, you learn about writing programs that use variables and arithmetic operators, and that receive interactive input from a user of your programs. We begin by reviewing variables and learning how to use them in a C++ program. You should do the exercises and labs in this chapter only after you have finished Chapter 1 of your book, *Programming Logic and Design, Fifth Edition*, by Joyce Farrell.

VARIABLES

As you know, a **variable** is a named location in the computer's memory whose contents can vary (thus the term variable). You use a variable in a program when you need to store values. The values stored in variables often change as a program executes.

In C++, you must declare variables before you can use them in a program. Declaring a variable is a two-part process: you give the variable a name, and you specify its data type. You'll learn about data types shortly. But first, we'll focus on the rules for naming variables in C++.

VARIABLE NAMES

Variable names in C++ can consist of letters, numerical digits, and the underscore character, but they cannot begin with a digit. Also, you cannot use a C++ keyword for a variable name. As you learned in Chapter 1 of this book, a keyword is a word with a special meaning in C++. The following are all examples of legal variable names in C++: `my_var`, `num6`, `intValue`, and `firstName`. Table 2-1 lists some examples of invalid variable names, and explains why each is invalid.

Name of Variable	Explanation
`3wrong`	Invalid because it begins with a digit
`$don't`	Invalid because it contains a single quotation mark and begins with a dollar sign
`int`	Invalid because it is a C++ keyword
`first name`	Invalid because it contains a space

Table 2-1 Invalid variable names

When naming variables, keep in mind that C++ is case sensitive—in other words, C++ knows the difference between uppercase and lowercase characters. That means `value`, `Value`, and `VaLuE` are three different variable names in C++.

In C++, variable names can be as long as you want. A good rule is to give variables meaningful names that are long enough to describe how the variable is used, but not so long that you make your program hard to read or cause yourself unnecessary typing. For example, a variable named `firstName` will clearly be used to store someone's first name. The variable name `freshmanStudentFirstName` is descriptive but inconveniently long; the variable name `fn` is too short to be meaningful at first glance. The variable name `x2rh5` is not meaningful.

C++ DATA TYPES

In addition to specifying a name for a variable, you also need to specify a particular data type for that variable. A variable's **data type** dictates the amount of memory that is allocated for the variable, the type of data that you can store in the variable, and the types of operations that can be performed using the variable. There are many different kinds of data types, but in this book we will focus on the most basic kind of data types, known as **primitive data types**. There are five primitive data types in C++: `int`, `float`, `double`, `char`, and `bool`. Some of these data types (such as `int`, `double`, and `float`) are used for variables that will store numeric values, and are referred to as numeric data types. The others have specialized purposes. For example, the `bool` data type is used to store a value of either true or false and the `char` data type is used to store a single character.

You will not use all of C++'s primitive data types in the programs you write in this book. Instead, you will focus on two of the numeric data types (`int` and `double`). The `int` data type is used for values that are whole numbers. For example, you could use a variable with the data type `int` to store someone's age (for example, 25) or the number of students in a class (for example, 35). A variable of the `int` data type consists of 32 bits (4 bytes) of space in memory. You use the data type `double` to store a floating-point value (that is, a fractional value), such as the price of an item in dollars and cents (2.95) or a measurement in feet or inches (2.5). A variable of the `double` data type consists of 64 bits (8 bytes) of space in memory. You will learn about using other data types as you continue to learn more about C++ in subsequent courses.

The `int` and `double` data types will be adequate for all the numeric variables you will use in this book. But what about when you need to store a group of characters (such as a person's name) in a variable? In programming, we refer to a group of one or more characters as a **string**. An example of a string is the last name "Wallace" or a product type such as a "desk". There is no primitive data type in C++ for storing strings; instead, they are stored in an object known as a `string` object. In addition to working with the `int` and `double` data types in this book, you will also work with `string`s.

》NOTE You used the `int` data type in Chapter 1 as the return type for the `main` function in the Hello World program.

》NOTE The actual size of the built-in data types may be different on different computers, but the sizes noted in this book indicate the usual sizes on a 32-bit computer.

》NOTE In *Programming Logic and Design, Fifth Edition,* data type num is used to refer to all numeric data types. A distinction is not made between `int` and `double` as it is in C++.

EXERCISE 2-1: USING C++ VARIABLES, DATA TYPES, AND KEYWORDS

In this exercise, you use what you have learned about naming C++ variables, C++ data types, and keywords to answer the following questions:

1. Is each of the following a legal C++ variable name? (Answer yes or no.)

my_age	_____	this_is_a_var	_____	NUMBER	_____
your_age	_____	number	_____	$number	_____
int	_____	number1	_____	floatNum	_____
25May	_____	number Six	_____	Number	_____

2. What data type (int, double, or string) is appropriate for storing each of the following values?

A product number _____

The amount of interest on a loan, such as 10% _____

The price of a CD _____

The name of your best friend _____

The number of books you own _____

DECLARING AND INITIALIZING VARIABLES

Now that you understand the rules for naming a variable, and you understand the concept of a data type, you are ready to learn how to declare a variable. In C++, you must declare all variables before you can use them in a program. When you **declare** a variable, you tell the compiler that you are going to use the variable. In the process of declaring a variable, you must specify the variable's name and its data type. Declaring a variable tells the compiler that it needs to reserve a memory location for the variable. A line of code that declares a variable is known as a **variable declaration**. The C++ syntax for a variable declaration is as follows:

```
dataType variableName;
```

For example, the following declaration statement declares a variable named counter of the int data type:

```
int counter;
```

The compiler reserves the amount of memory space allotted to an int variable (32 bits, or 4 bytes) for the variable named counter. The compiler then assigns the new variable a specific memory address. In Figure 2-1, the memory address for the variable named `counter` is 1000, although you wouldn't typically know the memory address of the variables included in your C++ programs.

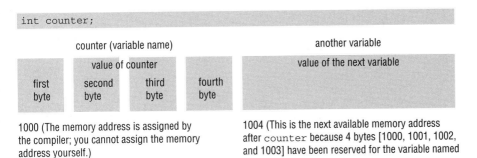

```
int counter;
```

counter (variable name)

value of counter

| first byte | second byte | third byte | fourth byte |

another variable

value of the next variable

1000 (The memory address is assigned by the compiler; you cannot assign the memory address yourself.)

1004 (This is the next available memory address after `counter` because 4 bytes [1000, 1001, 1002, and 1003] have been reserved for the variable named `counter`.)

Figure 2-1 Declaration of variable and memory allocation

You can also initialize a C++ variable when you declare it. When you **initialize** a C++ variable, you give it an initial value. For example, you can assign an initial value of 8 to the `counter` variable when you declare it, as shown in the following code:

```
int counter = 8;
```

You can also declare and initialize variables of data type `double` and `string` variables (objects) as shown in the following code:

```
double salary;
double cost = 12.95;
string firstName;
string homeAddress = "123 Main Street";
```

You can declare more than one variable in one statement as long as they have the same data type. For example, the following statement declares two variables, named `counter` and `value`. Both variables are of the `int` data type.

```
int counter, value;
```

> **» NOTE**
> In C++, variables are not automatically initialized with a value. They contain undetermined values unless you explicitly provide a value.

EXERCISE 2-2: DECLARING AND INITIALIZING C++ VARIABLES

In this exercise, you use what you have learned about declaring and initializing C++ variables.

1. Write a C++ variable declaration for each of the following. Use `int`, `double`, or `string` and choose meaningful variable names.

   Declare a variable to store an item number (1 to 1000). _____

   Declare a variable to store the number of children in your family. _____

Declare a variable to store the price of a pair of shoes. _____

Declare a variable to store the name of your favorite movie. _____

2. Declare and initialize variables to represent the following values. Use int, double, or string and choose meaningful variable names.

One leg of a triangle is 3.1 inches in length. _____

The number of days in March. _____

The name of your cat, "Puff". _____

The number of classes you are taking this term. _____

LAB 2-1: DECLARING AND INITIALIZING C++ VARIABLES

In this lab, you declare and initialize variables in a C++ program provided with the data files for this book. The program, which is saved in a file named NewAge.cpp, calculates your age in the year 2030.

1. Open the source code file named NewAge.cpp using Notepad or the text editor of your choice.

2. Declare an integer variable named myNewAge.

3. Declare and initialize an integer variable named myCurrentAge. Initialize this variable with your current age.

4. Declare and initialize an integer variable named currentYear. Initialize this variable with the value of the current year. Use four digits for the year.

5. Save this source code file in a directory of your choice, and then make that directory your working directory.

6. Compile the source code file NewAge.cpp.

7. Execute the program. Record the output of this program.

_____

_____

ARITHMETIC AND ASSIGNMENT OPERATORS

After you declare a variable, you can use it in various tasks. For example, you can use variables in simple arithmetic calculations, such as adding, subtracting, and multiplying. You can also perform other kinds of operations with variables, such as comparing one variable to another to determine which is greater.

In order to write C++ code that manipulates variables in this way, you need to be familiar with operators. An **operator** is a symbol that tells the computer to perform a mathematical or logical operation. C++ has a large assortment of operators. We begin the discussion with a group of operators known as the arithmetic operators.

ARITHMETIC OPERATORS

Arithmetic operators are the symbols used to perform arithmetic calculations. You are probably already very familiar with the arithmetic operators for addition (+) and subtraction (-). Table 2-2 lists and explains C++'s arithmetic operators.

Operator Name	Symbol	Example	Comment
Addition	+	num1 + num2	
Subtraction	–	num1 – num2	
Multiplication	*	num1 * num2	
Division	/	15/2	Integer division; result is 7; fraction is truncated.
		15.0 / 2.0	Floating point division; result is 7.5.
		15.0 / 2	Floating point division because one of the operands is a floating point number; result is 7.5.
Modulus	%	hours % 24	Performs division and finds the remainder; result is 1 if the value of hours is 25.
Unary plus	+	+num1	Maintains the value of the expression; if the value of num1 is 3, then +num1 is 3.
Unary minus	–	– (num1 – num2)	If value of (num1 – num2) is 10, then – (num1 – num2) is –10.

Table 2-2 C++ arithmetic operators

You can combine arithmetic operators and variables to create **expressions**. The computer evaluates each expression, and the result is a value. To give you an idea of how this works, assume that the value of num1 is 3 and num2 is 20, and that both are of data type int. With this information in mind, study the examples of expressions and their values in Table 2-3.

Expression	Value	Explanation
`num1 + num2`	23	because 3 + 20 = 23
`num1 - num2`	-17	because 3 - 20 = -17
`num2 % num1`	2	because 20 / 3 = 6 remainder 2
`num1 * num2`	60	because 3 * 20 = 60
`num2 / num1`	6	because 20 / 3 = 6 (remainder is truncated)
`-num1`	-3	because value of `num1` is 3, therefore `-num1` is -3

Table 2-3 Expressions and values

ASSIGNMENT OPERATORS AND THE ASSIGNMENT STATEMENT

Another type of operator is an assignment operator. You use an assignment operator to assign a value to a variable. A statement that assigns a value to a variable is known as an **assignment statement**. In C++, there are several types of assignment operators. The one you will use most often is the = assignment operator, which simply assigns a value to a variable. Table 2-4 lists and explains some of C++'s assignment operators.

Operator Name	Symbol	Example	Comment
Assignment	=	`count = 5;`	Places the value on the right side into the memory location named on the left side.
Initialization	=	`int count = 5;`	Places the value on the right side into the memory location named on the left side when the variable is declared.
Assignment	+=	`num += 20;`	Equivalent to `num = num + 20;`
	-=	`num -= 20;`	Equivalent to `num = num - 20;`
	*=	`num *= 20;`	Equivalent to `num = num * 20;`
	/=	`num /= 20;`	Equivalent to `num = num / 20;`
	%=	`num %= 20;`	Equivalent to `num = num % 20;`

Table 2-4 C++ assignment operators

When an assignment statement executes, the computer evaluates the expression on the right side of the assignment operator and then assigns the result to the memory location associated with the variable named on the left side of the assignment operator. An example of an assignment statement is shown in the following code. Notice that the statement ends with a semicolon. In C++, assignment statements always end with a semicolon.

```
answer = num1 * num2;
```

This assignment statement causes the computer to evaluate the expression num1 * num2. After evaluating the expression, the computer stores the results in the memory location associated with answer. If the value stored in the variable named num1 is 3, and the value stored in the variable named num2 is 20, then the value 60 is assigned to the variable named answer.

Here is another example:

```
answer += num1;
```

This statement is equivalent to the following statement:

```
answer = answer + num1;
```

If the value of answer is currently 10 and the value of num1 is 3, then the expression on the right side of the assignment statement answer + num1; evaluates to 13, and the computer assigns the value 13 to answer.

PRECEDENCE AND ASSOCIATIVITY

Once you start to write code that includes operators, you need to be aware of the order in which a series of operations is performed. In other words, you need to be aware of the **precedence** of operations in your code. Each operator is assigned a certain level of precedence. For example, multiplication has a higher level of precedence than addition. So in the expression 3 * 7 + 2, the 3 * 7 would be multiplied first; only after the multiplication was completed would the 2 be added.

But what happens when two operators have the same precedence? For example, 3 + 7 - 2. The rules of **associativity** determine the order in which operations are evaluated in an expression containing two or more operators with the same precedence. For example, in the expression 3 + 7 - 2, the addition and subtraction operators have the same precedence, so which operation will occur first? As shown in Table 2-5, the addition and subtraction operators have left-to-right associativity, which causes the expression to be evaluated from left to right (3 + 7 added first; then 2 is subtracted). Table 2-5 shows the precedence and associativity of the operators discussed in this chapter.

Operator Name	Operator Symbol(s)	Order of Precedence	Associativity
Parentheses	( )	First	Left to right
Unary	− +	Second	Right to left
Multiplication, division, and modulus	* / %	Third	Left to right
Addition and subtraction	+ −	Fourth	Left to right
Assignment	= += −+ *= /= %=	Fifth	Right to left

Table 2-5 Order of precedence and associativity

As you can see in Table 2-5, the parentheses operator, ( ), has the highest precedence. You use this operator to change the order in which operations are performed. Note the following example:

```
average = test1 + test2 / 2;
```

The task of this statement is to find the average of two test scores. The way this statement is currently written, the compiler will divide the value in the `test2` variable by 2, and then add it to the value in the `test1` variable. So, for example, if the value of `test1` is 90 and the value of `test2` is 88, then the value assigned to `average` will be 134, which is obviously not the correct average of these two test scores. By using the parentheses operator in this example, you can force the addition to occur before the division. The correct statement looks like this:

```
average = (test1 + test2) / 2;
```

In this example, the value of `test1`, 90, is added to the value of `test2`, 88, and then the sum is divided by 2. The value assigned to `average`, 89, is the correct result.

EXERCISE 2-3: UNDERSTANDING OPERATOR PRECEDENCE AND ASSOCIATIVITY

In this exercise, you use what you have learned about operator precedence and associativity in C++. Study the following code and then answer the subsequent questions.

```cpp
// This program demonstrates the precedence and
// associativity of operators.
#include <iostream>
using namespace std;
int main()
{
    int value1 = 9;
    int value2 = 3;
    int value3 = 10;
    int answer1, answer2, answer3;
    int answer4, answer5, answer6;

    answer1 = value1 * value2 + value3;
    cout << "Answer 1: " << answer1 << endl;

    answer2 = value1 * (value2 + value3);
    cout << "Answer 2: " << answer2 << endl;

    answer3 = value1 + value2 - value3;
    cout << "Answer 3: "<< answer3 << endl;

    answer4 = value1 + (value2 - value3);
    cout << "Answer 4: " << answer4 << endl;
```

```
    answer5 = value1 + value2 * value3;
    cout << "Answer 5: " << answer5 << endl;

    answer6 = value3 / value2;
    cout << "Answer 6: " << answer6 << endl;
    return 0;
}
```

1. What is the value of `answer1`, `answer2`, `answer3`, `answer4`, `answer5`, and
   `answer6`? _____

2. Explain how precedence and associativity affect the result.

   _____

   _____

   _____

   _____

   _____

LAB 2-2: ARITHMETIC AND ASSIGNMENT OPERATORS

In this lab, you complete a partially written C++ program that is provided along with the data
files for this book. The program, which was written for an appliance company, prints the
name of an appliance, its retail price, its wholesale price, the profit made on the appliance,
a sale price, and the profit made when the sale price is used.

1. Open the file named `Appliance.cpp` using Notepad or the text editor of your choice.

2. The file includes variable declarations and output statements. Read them carefully before
   you proceed to the next step.

3. Design the logic that will use assignment statements to first calculate the profit, then
   calculate the sale price, and finally calculate the profit when the sale price is used. Profit
   is defined as the retail price minus the wholesale price. The sale price is 15% deducted
   from the retail price. The sale profit is defined as the sale price minus the wholesale price.
   Perform the appropriate calculations as part of your assignment statements.

4. Save the source code file in a directory of your choice, and then make that directory your
   working directory.

5. Compile the program.

6. Execute the program. Your output should be as follows:

```
Item Name: Dishwasher
Retail Price: $425
Wholesale Price: $275
Profit: $150
Sale Price: $361.25
Sale Profit: $86.25
```

Next, you will see how to put together all you have learned in this chapter to write a C++ program that uses sequential statements and interactive input statements.

SEQUENTIAL STATEMENTS AND INTERACTIVE INPUT STATEMENTS

The term **sequential statements**, or **sequence**, refers to a series of statements that must be performed in sequential order, one after another. You use a sequence in programs when you want to perform actions one after the other. A sequence can contain any number of actions, but those actions must be in the proper order, and no action in the sequence can be skipped. Note that a sequence can contain comments, which are not considered part of the sequence itself. Comments serve as documentation, explaining the code to the programmer and any other people who might read it. You will learn more about comments in Chapter 3 of this book.

A sequence often includes **interactive input statements**, which are statements that ask, or **prompt**, the user to input data. The C++ program in the following example uses sequential statements and interactive input statements to convert a Fahrenheit temperature to its Celsius equivalent:

```cpp
// This C++ program converts a Fahrenheit temperature to Celsius.
// Input:  Interactive
// Output: Fahrenheit temperature followed by Celsius temperature

#include <iostream>
using namespace std;

int main()
{
    double fahrenheit;
    double celsius;

    // Prompt user
    cout << "Enter Fahrenheit temperature: ";
    // Get interactive user input
    cin >> fahrenheit;
    // Calculate celsius
    celsius = (fahrenheit - 32.0) * (5.0/9.0);
    // Output
```

```
    cout << "Fahrenheit temperature:" << fahrenheit << endl;
    cout << "Celsius temperature:" << celsius << endl;

    return 0;
}
```

This program is made up of sequential statements that execute one after the other. It also includes comments explaining the code. The comments are the lines that begin with //. After the variables `fahrenheit` and `celsius` are declared (using the `double` data type), the following statements execute:

```
// Prompt user
cout << "Enter Fahrenheit temperature: ";
// Get interactive user input
cin >> fahrenheit;
```

The `cout` statement is used to prompt the user for the Fahrenheit temperature so that the program can convert it to Celsius. Notice that `endl` is not included in this `cout` statement. This is done to position the cursor on the same line as the displayed prompt.

The next statement, `cin >> fahrenheit;`, is used to retrieve the user's input. This line consists of multiple parts. The first part, `cin`, is the name of an object that represents the user's standard input device, which is usually a keyboard. Next, you see >>, which is called the **extraction** or **input** operator. After >>, you see `fahrenheit`, which is the name of the variable that will store the data that is going to be extracted. The C++ extraction operator >> automatically converts input typed at the keyboard to the appropriate data type. In this example, >> will convert the user's input to the `double` data type because the variable `fahrenheit` is declared as data type `double`.

The next statement to execute is an assignment statement, as follows:

```
celsius = (fahrenheit - 32.0) * (5.0 / 9.0);
```

The formula that converts Fahrenheit temperatures to Celsius is used on the right side of this assignment statement. Notice the use of parentheses in the expression to control precedence. The expression is evaluated and the resulting value is assigned to the variable named `celsius`.

Notice that the division uses the values `5.0` and `9.0`. This is an example of floating-point division, which results in a value that includes a fraction. If the values 5 and 9 were used, integer division would be performed, and the fractional portion would be truncated.

The next two statements to execute in sequence are both output statements, as follows:

```
    cout << "Fahrenheit temperature:" << fahrenheit << endl;
    cout << "Celsius temperature:" << celsius << endl;
```

The statement `cout << Fahrenheit temperature: << fahrenheit << endl;` is used to display the string `Fahrenheit temperature:` followed by the value stored in the variable `fahrenheit`, followed by a newline character. The second output statement displays the words `Celsius temperature:` followed by the value stored in the variable `celsius`, followed by a newline character.

The last statement in this program is `return  0;`. As you learned in Chapter 1 of this book, this statement instructs the compiler to return the value 0 from the `main()` function.

Now that you have seen a complete C++ program that uses sequential statements and interactive input statements, it is time for you to begin writing your own programs.

EXERCISE 2-4: UNDERSTANDING SEQUENTIAL STATEMENTS

In this exercise, you use what you have learned about sequential statements to read a scenario and then you answer the subsequent questions. Suppose you have written a C++ program that calculates the amount of paint you need to cover the walls in your family room. Two walls are 9 feet high and 25.5 feet wide. The other two walls are 9 feet high and 22.2 feet wide. The salesperson at the home improvement store told you to buy 1 gallon of paint for every 200 square feet of wall you need to paint. Suppose you wrote the following code, but your program is not compiling. Take a few minutes to study this code and then answer Questions 1–2.

```cpp
// This program calculates the number of gallons of paint needed.
#include <iostream>
using namespace std;
int main()
{
    double height1 = 9;
    double height2 = 9;
    int width1 = 25.5;
    double width2 = 22.2;
    double squareFeet;
    int numGallons;
    numGallons = squareFeet / 200;
    squareFeet = (width1 * height1 + width2 * height2) * 2;
    cout << "Number of Gallons: " << numGallons << endl;
    return 0;
}
```

1. When you compile this program, you receive an error message from the `cl` compiler that is similar to the following:

   ```
   c:\users\jo ann\c++ pal\chapter_2\solutions\paint.cpp(12) : warning
   C4700: uninitialized local variable 'squareFeet' used
   ```

   There are multiple problems with this program even though the compiler issued only one error message, which is pointing out an uninitialized variable on line number 12 in the source code file. You would know the compiler is complaining about line 12 because of the `(12)` in the error message. On the following lines, describe how to fix all of the problems you can identify.

   _____

   _____

   _____

2. You have two variables declared in this program to represent the height of your walls, `height1` and `height2`. Do you need both of these variables? If not, how would you change the program? Be sure to identify all of the changes you would make.

_____

_____

_____

_____

_____

_____

LAB 2-3: USING SEQUENTIAL STATEMENTS IN A C++ PROGRAM

In this lab, you complete a C++ program provided with the data files for this book. The program calculates the amount of tax withheld from an employee's weekly salary, the tax deduction to which the employee is entitled for each dependent, and the employee's take-home pay. The program output includes state tax withheld, federal tax withheld, dependent tax deductions, salary, and take-home pay.

1. Open the source code file named `Payroll.cpp` using Notepad or the text editor of your choice.

2. Variables have been declared and initialized for you as needed and the input and output statements have been written. Read the code carefully before you proceed to the next step.

3. Write the C++ code needed to perform the following:

   Calculate state withholding tax at 7.0% and calculate federal withholding tax at 32.0%.

   Calculate dependent deductions at 4.0% of the employee's salary for each dependent.

   Calculate total withholding. (Total withholding is the total state withholding combined with the total federal withholding.)

   Calculate take-home pay as salary minus total withholding plus deductions.

4. Save this source code file in a directory of your choice, and then make that directory your working directory.

5. Compile the program.

» NOTE
You will learn how to control the number of places after the decimal point when you want to output floating-point values in Chapter 7 of this book.

6. Execute the program. You should get the following output:

State Tax: $66.5

Federal Tax: $304

Dependents: $114

Salary: $950

Take-Home Pay: $693.5

3

WRITING STRUCTURED C++ PROGRAMS

After studying this chapter, you will be able to:

Use structured flowcharts and pseudocode to write
    structured C++ programs
Write C++ comments
Write simple modular programs in C++, using local
    variables and named constants

In this chapter, you begin to learn how to write structured C++ programs. As you will see, creating a flowchart and writing pseudocode before you actually write the program ensures that you fully understand the program's intended design. We begin by looking at a structured flowchart and pseudocode from your text, *Programming Logic and Design, Fifth Edition*. You should do the exercises and labs in this chapter only after you have finished Chapters 2 and 3 of your book, *Programming Logic and Design, Fifth Edition*.

USING FLOWCHARTS AND PSEUDOCODE TO WRITE A C++ PROGRAM

In Chapters 1 and 2 of *Programming Logic and Design, Fifth Edition*, you studied flowcharts and pseudocode for the number-doubling program. Figure 3-1 shows the functional, structured flowchart and pseudocode for this program.

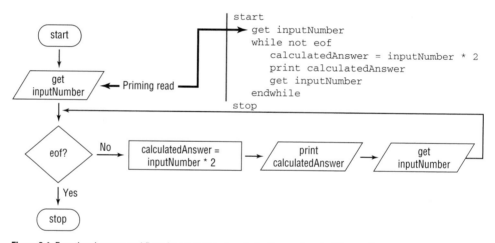

Figure 3-1 Functional, structured flowchart and pseudocode for the number-doubling problem

By studying the flowchart and pseudocode, you can see that this program makes use of the sequence and loop structures you have been introduced to in *Programming Logic and Design, Fifth Edition*. You must learn more about C++ before you can expect to write this program by yourself. The remainder of this section walks you through the C++ code for this program. The explanations assume that you are simply reading along; but if you want, you can type the code as it is presented. The goal of this section is to help you get a feel for how flowcharts and pseudocode can serve as a guide as you write C++ programs.

NOTE
Notice that each opening curly brace is matched by a closing curly brace.

In Figure 3-1, the first line of the pseudocode is the word `start`. How do we translate this pseudocode command into the C++ code that will start the number-doubling program? In Chapter 1 of this book, you learned that to start a C++ program, you first create a `main` function. So to start the number-doubling program, we will first create a function named main because it is always the first function that executes in a C++ program. Thus, the code that follows starts the number-doubling program by creating a main function:

```cpp
int main()
{
}
```

>> **NOTE** If you are typing the code as it is presented here, remember to save the program in a file that has an appropriate name, such as NumberDouble.cpp.

The next line of the pseudocode instructs you to get the inputNumber. In other words, you need to write the input statement that primes the loop. You learned about priming read statements in Chapter 2 of *Programming Logic and Design, Fifth Edition*. In Chapter 2 of this book, you learned how to use interactive input statements in programs to allow the user to input data. You also learned to prompt the user to explain what the program expects to receive as input. The following example includes the code that implements the priming read by displaying a prompt for the user and then retrieving the number the user wants to be doubled.

Note that the code in boldface has been added to the number-doubling program. If you were writing this code yourself, you would start by writing the code for the number-doubling program as shown above, and then edit it to add the boldface code shown here:

```cpp
int main()
{
    cout << "Enter a number to double: " << endl;
    cin >> inputNumber;
}
```

Next, the pseudocode instructs you to begin a while loop with eof (end of file) used as the condition to exit the loop.

Since we are using interactive input in this program, it requires no eof marker. Instead we will use the number 0 (zero) to indicate the end of input. We'll use 0 because 0 doubled will always be 0. The use of 0 to indicate the end of input also requires us to change the prompt to tell the user how to end the program. Review the following code. Again, the newly added code is formatted in bold.

```cpp
int main()
{
    cout << "Enter a number to double or 0 to end: " << endl;
    cin >> inputNumber;
    while( inputNumber != 0)
    {
    }
}
```

>> **NOTE**
You have not learned enough about while loops to write this code yourself, but you can observe how it is done in this example. You will learn more about loops in Chapter 5 of this book.

According to the pseudocode, the body of the loop is made up of three sequential statements. The first statement calculates the inputNumber multiplied by 2; the second statement prints the calculatedAnswer; and the third statement retrieves the next inputNumber from the user. In C++, we actually need to add an additional statement between the curly braces that mark the body of the while loop. This additional statement prompts the user to enter the next number to be doubled.

In the following example, the code that makes up the body of the loop is in bold:

```
int main()
{
   cout << "Enter a number to double or 0 to end: " << endl;
   cin >> inputNumber;
   while( inputNumber != 0)
   {
      calculatedAnswer = inputNumber * 2;
      cout << inputNumber << " doubled is " << calculatedAnswer << endl;
      cout << "Enter a number to double or 0 to end: " << endl;
      cin >> inputNumber;

   }
}
```

The last line of the pseudocode instructs you to end the program. In C++, the closing curly brace (}) for the main function signifies the end of the main function and therefore the end of the program. Note that the preceding code includes two closing curly braces. The last one is the one that ends the main function and the second to last one ends the while loop.

We are almost finished translating the pseudocode into C++ code. We just have a few housekeeping tasks to take care of. As you learned in Chapter 3 of *Programming Logic and Design, Fifth Edition*, declaring variables is one of these housekeeping tasks. The code that follows is the completed C++ program for doubling numbers. The code shown in bold is the code that declares the variables. The #include preprocessor directive and the using statement that you learned about in Chapter 1 of this book are also shown in bold. Additionally, you see the return 0; statement. This statement instructs the compiler to return the value 0 from the main function.

```
#include <iostream>
using namespace std;
int main()
{
   int inputNumber;
   int calculatedAnswer;
   cout << "Enter a number to double or 0 to end: " << endl;
   cin >> inputNumber;
   while( inputNumber != 0)
   {
      calculatedAnswer = inputNumber * 2;
      cout << inputNumber << " doubled is " << calculatedAnswer << endl;
      cout << "Enter a number to double or 0 to end: " << endl;
      cin >> inputNumber;

   }
   return 0;
}
```

At this point, the program is ready to be compiled. Assuming there are no syntax errors, it should execute as planned. Although you have not learned everything you need to know to write this program yourself, you can see from this example that if you start with a well designed, functional, structured flowchart or pseudocode, writing the program in C++ is easier.

LAB 3-1: USING FLOWCHARTS AND PSEUDOCODE TO WRITE A C++ PROGRAM

In this lab, you use the flowchart and pseudocode in Figure 3-2 to add code to a partially created C++ program. When completed, college admissions officers should be able to use the C++ program to determine whether to accept or reject a student, based on his or her class rank. You studied this flowchart and pseudocode in Chapter 2 of your book, *Programming Logic and Design, Fifth Edition*.

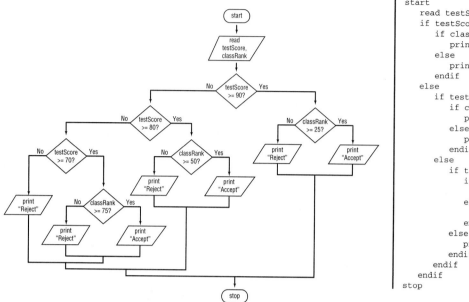

```
start
   read testScore, classRank
   if testScore >= 90 then
      if classRank >= 25 then
         print "Accept"
      else
         print "Reject"
      endif
   else
      if testScore >= 80 then
         if classRank >= 50 then
            print "Accept"
         else
            print "Reject"
         endif
      else
         if testScore >= 70 then
            if classRank >= 75 then
               print "Accept"
            else
               print "Reject"
            endif
         else
            print "Reject"
         endif
      endif
   endif
stop
```

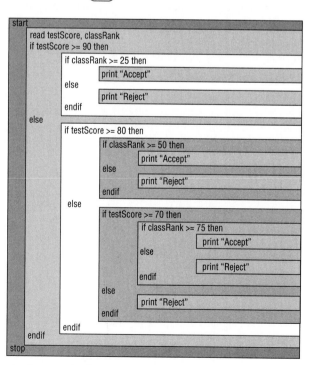

Figure 3-2 Flowchart and pseudocode of structured college admission program

1. Study the flowchart and pseudocode in Figure 3-2.

2. Open the source code file named `CollegeAdmission.cpp` using Notepad or the text editor of your choice.

3. Declare two integer variables named `testScore` and `classRank`.

4. Write the interactive input statements to retrieve a student's test score and class rank from the user of the program. Don't forget to prompt the user for the test score and class rank.

5. The rest of the program is written for you. Save this source code file in a directory of your choice, and then make that directory your working directory.

6. Compile the source code file `CollegeAdmission.cpp`.

7. Execute the program by entering 75 for the test score and 80 for the class rank. Record the output of this program.

    _____

8. Execute the program by entering 80 for the test score and 40 for the class rank. Record the output of this program.

    _____

C++ COMMENTS

In Chapter 3 of your book, *Programming Logic and Design, Fifth Edition*, you learned about **program comments**, which are statements that do not execute. You use comments in C++ programs to explain your logic to people who read your source code. The C++ compiler ignores comments.

You can choose from two commenting styles in C++. In the first, you type two forward slash characters (//) at the beginning of each comment that you want the compiler to ignore. This style is useful when you only want to mark a single line or part of a line as a comment. In the second style, you enclose a block of lines with the characters /* and */. This style is useful when you want to mark several lines as a comment. You may place comments anywhere in a C++ program except within a statement.

The following example shows both styles of comments added to the number-doubling program from the previous section. Note that the first eight lines of the program make up a multiline, block comment that explains some basic information about the program.

A second block comment follows this first one, introducing the code that creates the number-doubling program. Next, several single-line comments are included throughout to describe various parts of the program.

>> NOTE
It is a good programming practice to include header comments that provide basic information about a program.

```cpp
/*
    Program Name: NumberDouble.cpp
    Function: This program doubles a number that is input by
    a user and prints the calculated result on the user's
    screen.
    Input:   Interactive
    Output: The doubled number
*/
#include <iostream>
using namespace std;

/*
The following code creates the number-doubling program. It has a single
function named main.
*/
int main()
{
    // Declaration of variables
    int inputNumber;
    int calculatedAnswer;

    // Prompt user and get interactive user input
    cout << "Enter a number to double: " << endl;
    cin >> inputNumber;

    // Continue until user enters a 0 to end the program
    while( inputNumber != 0)
    {
      // Calculate the number doubled
      calculatedAnswer = inputNumber * 2;
      // Output the result
      cout << inputNumber << " doubled is " << calculatedAnswer << endl;
      // Prompt user and get interactive user input
      cout << "Enter a number to double: " << endl;
      cin >> inputNumber;
    } // End of while loop
    return 0;
} // End of main function
```

▶▶ NOTE You are responsible for including well-written, meaningful comments in all of the programs that you write. In fact, some people think that commenting your source code is as important as the source code itself.

Next, you will see how to use a flowchart and pseudocode to write a modular program in C++.

LAB 3-2: COMMENTING C++ PROGRAMS

In this lab, you add comments to a previously created C++ program. This C++ program finds the sum of the numbers from 0 to 100 that are divisible by 13. Study the code to see if you can figure out what each line of code does, and then add comments to the code that include a multiline comment similar to that in the number-doubling program that describes what the program does and any other comments you think appropriate. Use the programs you have seen thus far in this book to help you.

1. Open the source code file named `DivideByThirteen.cpp` using Notepad or the text editor of your choice.

2. Study the code.

3. Add your comments.

4. Save this source code file in a directory of your choice, and then make that directory your working directory.

5. Compile the source code file `DivideByThirteen.cpp`.

6. Execute the program. Record the output of this program.

WRITING A MODULAR PROGRAM IN C++

In Chapter 3 of your book, *Programming Logic and Design, Fifth Edition*, you learned about local variables and named constants. Briefly, you declare **local variables** within the module—or, in C++ terminology, the function—that uses them. Further, you can only use a local variable within the function in which it is declared. (Note that in this book, we'll use the term "function" when referring to a C++ program as this is the term used in the C++ programming language. When referring to a flowchart or pseudocode, the term "module" is used.) You use **named constants** in programs where the value assigned will never change as the program executes.

Also, recall from Chapter 3 that most programs consist of a main method that contains the mainline logic. The main method then calls other methods to get specific work done in the program.

In Chapter 3 of *Programming Logic and Design, Fifth Edition*, you studied a flowchart and pseudocode for a modular program that prints a customer bill with variables and constants declared locally in each method. This flowchart and pseudocode are shown in Figure 3-3.

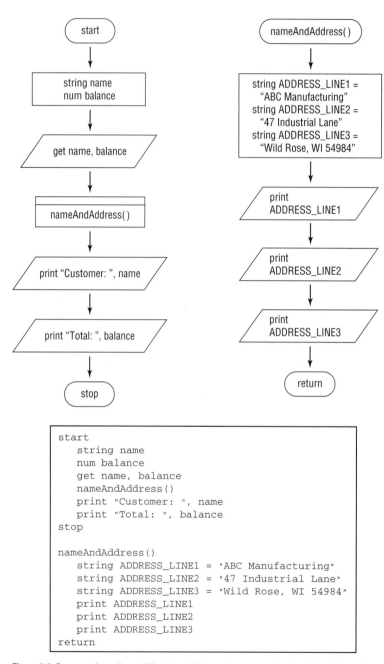

```
start
   string name
   num balance
   get name, balance
   nameAndAddress()
   print "Customer: ", name
   print "Total: ", balance
stop

nameAndAddress()
   string ADDRESS_LINE1 = "ABC Manufacturing"
   string ADDRESS_LINE2 = "47 Industrial Lane"
   string ADDRESS_LINE3 = "Wild Rose, WI 54984"
   print ADDRESS_LINE1
   print ADDRESS_LINE2
   print ADDRESS_LINE3
return
```

Figure 3-3 Program that prints a bill with variables and constants declared locally in each method

In this section, we walk through the process of creating a C++ program that implements the logic illustrated in the flowchart in Figure 3-3. According to the flowchart, the program begins with the execution of the mainline method. The mainline method declares two variables, name and balance, that are local to the mainline method. Next, values for name and balance are retrieved using an input statement. To translate this into C++, we need to declare three variables, firstName, lastName, and balance, and then we use interactive input statements to retrieve the user-entered values for name and balance.

After the input statements, the function named nameAndAddress is called. The last two statements in the mainline logic are print statements that output the customer's name and balance. In the C++ version of the program, the output appears on (is printed to) the user's screen. In the following code, the mainline logic for this program is translated into C++.

```cpp
/* Program Name: CustomerBill.cpp
   Function: This program uses a function to print a company name and
   address and then prints a customer name and balance.
   Input:  Interactive
   Output: Company name and address, customer name and balance
*/
#include <iostream>
#include <string>
using namespace std;
int main()
{
   // Declare variables local to main
   string firstName;
   string lastName;
   double balance;
   // Get interactive input
   cout << "Enter customer's first name: ";
   cin >> firstName;
   cout << "Enter customer's last name: ";
   cin >> lastName;
   cout << "Enter customer's balance: ";
   cin >> balance;
   // Call nameAndAddress function
   nameAndAddress();
   // Output customer name and address
   cout << "Customer Name:  " << firstName << " " << lastName << endl;
   cout << "Customer Balance:  " << balance << endl;
   return 0;
} // End of main function
```

» NOTE If you are typing the code as it is presented here, remember to save the program in a file that has a meaningful name, such as CustomerBill.cpp.

To complete this program, we need to add the function named nameAndAddress. Looking at the flowchart in Figure 3-3, you see that we need to declare the three constants that are local to the nameAndAddress function: ADDRESS_LINE1, ADDRESS_LINE2, and ADDRESS_LINE3. The flowchart tells us that the program should then print these three constant values. In this program, we print these values on the user's screen. In the following example, the code that implements the nameAndAddress function has been added to the CustomerBill program. The new code is shown in bold.

```cpp
/* Program Name: CustomerBill.cpp
   Function: This program uses a function to print a company name and
   address and then prints a customer name and balance.
   Input:  Interactive
   Output: Company name and address, customer name and balance
*/
#include <iostream>
#include <string>
void nameAndAddress(); // function declaration
using namespace std;
int main()
{
   // Declare variables local to main
   string firstName;
   string lastName;
   double balance;
   // Get interactive input
   cout << "Enter customer's first name: ";
   cin >> firstName;
   cout << "Enter customer's last name: ";
   cin >> lastName;
   cout << "Enter customer's balance: ";
   cin >> balance;
   // Call nameAndAddress function
   nameAndAddress();
   // Output customer name and address
   cout << "Customer Name:  " << firstName << " " << lastName <<endl;
   cout << "Customer Balance:  " << balance << endl;
   return 0;
} // End of main function
void nameAndAddress()
{
   // Declare and initialize local, constant strings
   const string ADDRESS_LINE1 = "ABC Manufacturing";
   const string ADDRESS_LINE2 = "47 Industrial Lane";
   const string ADDRESS_LINE3 = "Wild Rose, WI 54984";

   // Output
   cout << ADDRESS_LINE1 << endl;
   cout << ADDRESS_LINE2 << endl;
   cout << ADDRESS_LINE3 << endl;
}  // End of nameAndAddress function
```

Looking at the code, you see that in order to declare a constant in C++, you use the keyword const, followed by the data type, followed by the name of the constant. Named constants must be initialized when they are declared and their contents may not be changed during the execution of the program. The three named constants, ADDRESS_LINE1, ADDRESS_LINE2, and ADDRESS_LINE3, are local to the function nameAndAddress because they are declared within the function. An opening curly brace ({) marks the beginning of the function and a closing curly brace (}) marks the end.

The **header** for the method, nameAndAddress, begins with the keyword void, followed by the function name, which is nameAndAddress. The keyword void indicates that the nameAndAddress function does not return a value.

Notice that an additional #include preprocessor directive has been added at the beginning of the program. The preprocessor directive #include <string> allows you to use string objects in your C++ program. You will learn more about string objects in subsequent chapters. Also, notice the statement that follows the #include preprocessor directives, void nameAndAddress();. This is called a function declaration or function prototype.

In C++, you must declare all functions that are used in your program before you may call them. A **function declaration** specifies the data type of the value the function returns, the function name, and the data type of any arguments that are passed to the function. The nameAndAddress function returns the data type void. The keyword void is used to specify that this function returns nothing. You will learn more about function declarations and function arguments in Chapter 7 of this book.

This program is now complete. Figure 3-4 shows the program's output in response to the input William Pryor (for the name), and 1200 (for the balance).

>>**NOTE**
By convention, in C++ the names of constants appear in all uppercase letters. Multiple words are separated with underscores. This makes it easier for you to spot named constants in a long block of code.

>>**NOTE**
Function declarations end with a semicolon (;).

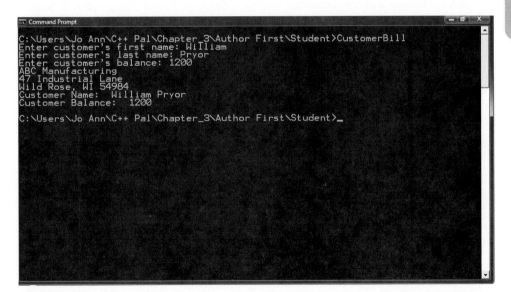

Figure 3-4 Output of the CustomerBill program when the input is William Pryor and 1200

LAB 3-3: WRITING A MODULAR PROGRAM IN C++

In this lab, you add the input and output statements to a partially completed C++ program. When completed, the user should be able to enter a year, a month, and a day. The program then determines if the date is valid. Valid years are those that are greater than 0, valid months include the values 1 through 12, and valid days include the values 1 through 31.

1. Open the source code file named `BadDate.cpp` using Notepad or the text editor of your choice.

2. Notice that variables have been declared for you.

3. Write prompts and input statements to retrieve a year, a month, and a day from the user.

4. Write the output statements. The format of the output is as follows:

    ```
    month/day/year is a valid date.
    ```

    or

    ```
    month/day/year is an invalid date.
    ```

5. Save this source code file in a directory of your choice, and then make that directory your working directory.

6. Compile the source code file `BadDate.cpp`.

7. Execute the program entering the following date: month = 10, day = 17, year = 2009. Record the output of this program.

    _____

    Execute the program entering the following date: month = 2, day = 32, year = 2006. Record the output of this program.

    _____

4

WRITING PROGRAMS
THAT MAKE DECISIONS

After studying this chapter, you will be able to:

Use relational and logical Boolean operators to make
   decisions in a program

Compare `string` objects

Write decision statements in C++, including
   an `if` statement, an `if-else` statement, nested
   `if` statements, and the `switch` statement

Use decision statements to make multiple comparisons
   by using AND logic and OR logic

You should complete the exercises and labs in this chapter only after you have finished Chapter 4 of your book, *Programming Logic and Design, Fifth Edition*, by Joyce Farrell. In this chapter, you practice using C++'s relational and logical operators to write Boolean expressions. You also learn the C++ syntax for decision statements, including the `if` statement, the `if-else` statement, nested `if` statements, and `switch` statements. Finally, you learn to write C++ statements that make multiple comparisons.

BOOLEAN OPERATORS

You use Boolean operators in expressions when you want to compare values in an expression. When you use a Boolean operator in an expression, the evaluation of that expression results in a value that is `true` or `false`. In C++, you can subdivide the **Boolean operators** into two groups: relational operators and logical operators. We begin the discussion with the relational operators.

RELATIONAL OPERATORS

In the context of programming, the term **relational** refers to the connections, or relationships, between values. For example, one value might be greater than another, less than another, or equal to the other value. The terms "greater than," "less than," and "equal to" all refer to a relationship between two values. As with all Boolean operators, a **relational operator** allows you to ask a question that results in a `true` or `false` answer. Depending on the answer, your program will execute different statements that can perform different actions.

Table 4-1 lists the relational operators used in C++.

Operator	Meaning
<	Less than
<=	Less than or equal to
>	Greater than
>=	Greater than or equal to
==	Equal to (two equal signs with no space between them)
!=	Not equal to

Table 4-1 Relational operators

To see how to use relational operators, suppose you declare two variables: an `int` named `number1` that you initialize with the value `10` and another `int` variable named `number2` that you initialize with the value `15`. The following code shows the declaration statements for these variables:

```
int number1 = 10;
int number2 = 15;
```

The following code samples illustrate how relational operators are used in expressions:

» `number1 < number2` evaluates to `true` because 10 is less than 15.

» `number1 <= number2` evaluates to `true` because 10 is less than or equal to 15.

» `number1 > number2` evaluates to `false` because 10 is not greater than 15.

» `number1 >= number2` evaluates to `false` because 10 is not greater than or equal to 15.

» `number1 == number2` evaluates to `false` because 10 is not equal to 15.

» `number1 != number2` evaluates to `true` because 10 is not equal to 15.

LOGICAL OPERATORS

You can use another type of Boolean operator, **logical operators**, when you need to ask more than one question but you want to receive only one answer. For example, in a program, you may want to ask if a number is between the values 1 and 10. This actually involves two questions. You need to ask if the number is greater than 1 AND if the number is less than 10. Here, you are asking two questions but you want only one answer—either yes (`true`) or no (`false`).

Like statements that contain relational expressions, statements that contain logical operators evaluate to `true` or `false`, thereby permitting decision-making in your programs.

Table 4-2 lists the logical operators used in C++.

Operator	Name	Description
`&&`	AND	All expressions must evaluate to `true` for the entire expression to be `true`; this operator is written as two `&` symbols with no space between them.
`||`	OR	Only one expression must evaluate to `true` for the entire expression to be `true`; this operator is written as two `|` symbols with no space between them.
`!`	NOT	This operator reverses the value of the expression; for example, if the expression evaluates to `false`, then reverse it so that the expression evaluates to `true`.

Table 4-2 Logical operators

To see how to use the logical operators, suppose you declare two variables: an `int` named `number1` that you initialize with the value 10; and another `int` variable named `number2` that you initialize with the value 15. The declaration statements for these variables are shown in the following code:

```
int number1 = 10;
int number2 = 15;
```

The following code samples illustrate how you can use the logical operators along with the relational operators in expressions:

» `(number1 > number2) || (number1 == 10)` evaluates to `true` because the first expression evaluates to `false`, 10 is not greater than 15, and the second expression evaluates to `true`, 10 is equal to 10. Only one expression needs to be `true` using OR logic for the entire expression to be `true`.

» `(number1 > number2) && (number1 == 10)` evaluates to `false` because the first expression is `false`, 10 is not greater than 15, and the second expression is `true`, 10 is equal to 10. Using AND logic, both expressions must be `true` for the entire expression to be `true`.

» `(number1 != number2) && (number1 == 10)` evaluates to `true` because both expressions are `true`; that is, 10 is not equal to 15 and 10 is equal to 10. Using AND logic, if both expressions are `true`, then the entire expression is `true`.

» `!(number1 == number2)` evaluates to `true` because the expression evaluates to `false`, 10 is not equal to 15. The `!` operator then reverses `false`, which results in a `true` value.

RELATIONAL AND LOGICAL OPERATOR PRECEDENCE AND ASSOCIATIVITY

Like the arithmetic operators discussed in Chapter 2, the relational and logical operators are evaluated according to specific rules of associativity and precedence. Table 4-3 shows the precedence and associativity of the operators discussed thus far in this book.

Operator Name	Operator Symbol(s)	Order of Precedence	Associativity
Parentheses	( )	First	Left to right
Unary	− + !	Second	Right to left
Multiplication, division, and modulus	* / %	Third	Left to right
Addition and subtraction	+ −	Fourth	Left to right
Relational	< > <= >=	Fifth	Left to right
Equality	== !=	Sixth	Left to right
AND	&&	Seventh	Left to right
OR	||	Eighth	Left to right
Assignment	= += −+ *= /= %=	Ninth	Right to left

Table 4-3 Order of precedence and associativity

» **NOTE** Some symbols appear in Table 4-3 more than once because they have more than one meaning. For example, when the − operator is used before a number or a variable that contains a number, it is interpreted as the unary − operator. When the − operator is used between operands, it is interpreted as the subtraction operator.

As shown in Table 4-3, the AND operator has a higher **precedence** than the OR operator, meaning its Boolean values are evaluated first. Also notice that the relational operators have higher precedence than the equality operators and both the relational and equality operators have higher precedence than the AND and OR operators. All of these operators have left-to-right associativity.

To see how to use the logical operators and the relational operators in expressions, first assume that the variables number1 and number2 are declared and initialized as shown in the following code:

```
int number1 = 10;
int number2 = 15;
```

Now, you write the following expression in C++:

```
number1 == 8 && number2 == number1 || number2 == 15
```

Looking at Table 4-3, you can see that the equality operator (==) has a higher level of precedence than the AND operator (&&) and the AND operator (&&) has a higher level of precedence than the OR operator (||). Also, notice that there are three == operators in the expression; thus, the left-to-right associativity rule applies. Figure 4-1 illustrates the order in which the operators are used.

```
int number1 = 10;
int number2 = 15;
```

number1 == 8 && number2 == number1 || number2 == 15

| Step 1 false | | Step 2 false | | Step 3 true |

&&

Step 4 false

||

Step 5 true

Figure 4-1 Evaluation of expression using relational and logical operators

NOTE
Remember that you can change the order of precedence by using parentheses.

As you can see in Figure 4-1, it takes five steps, following the rules of precedence and associativity, to determine the value of the expression.

As you can see in Figure 4-2, when parentheses are added, it still takes five steps, but the order of evaluation is changed and the result is also changed.

```
int number1 = 10;
int number2 = 15;
```

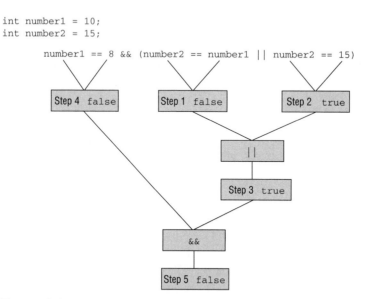

Figure 4-2 Evaluation of expression using relational and logical operators with parentheses

COMPARING STRINGS

In C++, you may use the same relational operators when you compare string objects that you use to compare numeric data types such as ints and doubles.

The following code shows how to use the equality operator to compare two string objects and also to compare one string object and one string constant:

```
string s1 = "Hello";
string s2 = "World";
// The following test evaluates to false because "Hello" is not the
// same as "World".
if (s1 == s2)
    // code written here executes if true
else
    // code written here executes if false

// The following test evaluates to true because "Hello" is the same
// as "Hello".
if (s1 == "Hello")
    // code written here executes if true
else
    // code written here executes if false
```

```
// The following test evaluates to false because "Hello" is not the
// same as "hello".
if (s1 == "hello")
    // code written here executes if true
else
    // code written here executes if false
```

>> NOTE
Two strings are
equal when their
contents are the
same.

>> **NOTE** C++ is **case sensitive**, which means that C++ does not consider a lowercase "h" to be equal to an uppercase "H" because their ASCII values are different. Lowercase "h" has an ASCII value of 104 and uppercase "H" has an ASCII value of 72. A table of ASCII values can be found in Appendix C - Understanding Numbering Systems and Computer Codes in *Programming Logic and Design, Fifth Edition*.

The following code shows how to use the other relational operators to compare two `string` objects and also to compare one `string` object and one `string` constant:

```
string s1 = "Hello";
string s2 = "World";
// The following test evaluates to false because "Hello" is not
// greater than "World".
if (s1 > s2)
    // code written here executes if true
else
    // code written here executes if false

// The following test evaluates to true because "Hello" is the same as
// "Hello".
if (s1 <= "Hello")
    // code written here executes if true
else
    // code written here executes if false
```

When you compare `strings`, C++ compares the ASCII values of the individual characters in the `string` to determine if one `string` is greater than, less than, or equal to another, in terms of alphabetizing the text in the `strings`. As shown in the preceding code, the `string` object s1, whose value is `"Hello"`, is not greater than the `string` object s2, whose value is `"World"`, because `World` comes after `Hello` in alphabetical order.

The following code sample shows additional examples of using the relational operators with two `string` objects:

```
string s1 = "whole";
string s2 = "whale";
// The next statement evaluates to true because the contents of
// s1, "whole", are greater than the contents of s2, "whale".
if (s1 > s2)
    // code written here executes if true
else
    // code written here executes if false
```

```
// The next statement evaluates to true because the contents of s2,
// "whale", are less than the contents of s1, "whole".
if (s2 < s1)
    // code written here executes if true
else
    // code written here executes if false

// The next statement evaluates to true because the contents of s1,
// "whole", are the same as the string constant, "whole".
if (s1 == "whole")
    // code written here executes if true
else
    // code written here executes if false
```

DECISION STATEMENTS

Every decision in a program is based on whether an expression evaluates to `true` or `false`. Programmers use decision statements to change the flow of control in a program. **Flow of control** means the order in which statements are executed. Decision statements are also known as branching statements because they cause the computer to make a decision, choosing from one or more branches (or paths) in the program.

There are different types of decision statements in C++. We will begin with the `if` statement.

THE IF STATEMENT

The `if` statement is a single-path decision statement. As you learned in *Programming Logic and Design, Fifth Edition*, `if` statements are also referred to as "single alternative" or "single-sided" statements.

When we use the term "single-path," we mean that if an expression evaluates to `true`, your program executes one or more statements; but if the expression evaluates to `false`, your program will not execute these statements. There is only one defined path—the path taken if the expression evaluates to `true`. In either case, the statement following the `if` statement is executed.

The syntax, or set of rules, for writing an `if` statement in C++ is as follows:

```
if(expression)
    statementA;
```

Note that when you type the keyword `if` to begin an `if` statement, you follow it with an expression placed within parentheses.

When the compiler encounters an `if` statement, the expression within the parentheses is evaluated. If the expression evaluates to `true`, then the computer executes *statementA*. If the expression in parentheses evaluates to `false`, then the computer will not execute *statementA*. Remember that whether the expression evaluates to `true` and executes *statementA*, or the expression evaluates to `false` and does not execute *statementA*, the statement following the `if` executes next.

Note that a C++ statement, such as an `if` statement, can be either a simple statement or a block statement. A **block** statement is made up of multiple C++ statements. C++ defines a block as statements placed within a pair of curly braces. If you want your program to execute more than one statement as part of an `if` statement, you must enclose the statements in a pair of curly braces or only one statement will execute. The following example illustrates an `if` statement that uses the relational operator < to test if the value of the variable `customerAge` is less than 65. You will see the first curly brace in the fourth line and the second curly brace in the third to seventh line.

```cpp
int customerAge = 53;
int discount = 10, numUnder_65 = 0;
if(customerAge < 65)
{
    discount = 0;
    numUnder_65 += 1;
}
cout << "Discount : " << discount << endl;
cout << "Number of customers under 65 is: " << numUnder_65 << endl;
```

In the preceding code, the variable named `customerAge` is initialized to the value 53. Because 53 is less than 65, the expression `customerAge < 65` evaluates to `true` and the block statement executes. The block statement is made up of the two assignment statements within the curly braces: `discount = 0;` and `numUnder_65 += 1;`. If the expression evaluates to `false`, the block statement does not execute. In either case, the next statement to execute is the output statement `cout << "Discount : " << discount << endl;`.

Notice that you do not include a semicolon at the end of the line with the `if` and the expression to be tested. Doing so is not a syntax error, but it can create a logic error in your program. A **logic error** causes your program to produce incorrect results. In C++, the semicolon (`;`) is called the null statement and is considered a legal statement. The **null** statement is a statement that does nothing. Examine the following code:

```cpp
if (customerAge < 65); // semicolon here is not correct
{
    discount = 0;
    numUnder_65 += 1;
}
```

If you write an `if` statement as shown in the preceding code, your program will test the expression `customerAge < 65`. If it evaluates to `true`, the null statement executes, which means your program does nothing, and then the statement `discount = 0;` executes because this is the next statement following the `if` statement. This does not cause a logic error in your program, but consider what happens when the expression in the `if` statement evaluates to `false`. If `false`, the null statement does not execute, but the statement `discount = 0;` will execute because it is the next statement after the `if` statement.

The following code uses an `if` statement to test two `string` objects for equality:

```cpp
string dentPlan = "Y";
if (dentPlan == "Y")
    grossPay = grossPay - 23.50;
```

In this example, if the value of the `string` object named `dentPlan` and the string constant `"Y"` are the same value, the expression evaluates to `true`, and the `grossPay` calculation assignment statement executes. If the expression evaluates to `false`, the `grossPay` calculation assignment statement does not execute.

EXERCISE 4-1: UNDERSTANDING IF STATEMENTS

In this exercise, you use what you have learned about writing `if` statements in C++ to study a complete C++ program that uses `if` statements. Take a few minutes to study the code that follows, and then answer Questions 1 through 4.

```cpp
// VotingAge.cpp - This program determines if a
// person is eligible to vote.
#include <iostream>
#include <string>
using namespace std;
int main()
{
    int myAge = 19;
    string ableToVote = "Yes";
    const int VOTING_AGE = 18;
    if(myAge < VOTING_AGE)
        ableToVote = "No";
    cout << "My Age: " <<  myAge << endl;
    cout << "Able To Vote: " << ableToVote << endl;
    return 0;
}
```

1. What is the exact output when this program executes?

   _____

   _____

2. What is the exact output if the value of `myAge` is changed to 17?

   _____

   _____

3. What is the exact output if the expression in the `if` statement is changed to `myAge <= VOTING_AGE`?

   _____

   _____

4. What is the exact output if the variable named `ableToVote` is initialized with the value "No" rather than the value "Yes"?

   _____

   _____

LAB 4-1: USING IF STATEMENTS

In this lab, you complete a prewritten C++ program for a furniture company. The program is supposed to compute the price of any table a customer orders, based on the following facts:

» The charge for all tables is a minimum of $150.00.

» If the surface (length * width) is over 750 square inches, add $50.00.

» If the wood is mahogany, add $200.00; for oak add $100.00. No charge is added for pine.

» For extension leaves for the table, there is an additional $50.00 charge each.

1. Open the file named Furniture.cpp using Notepad or the text editor of your choice.

2. You need to declare variables for the following, and initialize them where specified:

» A variable for the cost of the table initialized to 0.00.

» A variable for the length of the table initialized to 50 inches.

» A variable for the width of the table initialized to 40 inches.

» A variable for the surface area of the table.

» A variable for the wood type initialized with the value "oak".

» A variable for the number of extension leaves initialized with the value 2.

3. Write the rest of the program using assignment statements and if statements as appropriate. The output statements are written for you.

4. Compile the program.

5. Execute the program. Your output should be: The charge for this table is $400. Note that you cannot control the number of places that appear after the decimal point until you learn more about C++ in Chapter 7 of this book.

THE IF-ELSE STATEMENT

The if-else statement is a dual-path or dual-alternative decision statement. That is, your program will take one of two paths as a result of evaluating an expression in an if-else statement.

The syntax for writing an if-else statement in C++ is as follows:

```
if (expression)
    statementA;
else
    statementB;
```

When the compiler encounters an if-else statement, the expression in the parentheses is evaluated. If the expression evaluates to true, then the computer executes statementA. Otherwise, if the expression in parentheses evaluates to false, then the computer executes statementB. Both statementA and statementB can be simple statements or block statements. Regardless of which path is taken in a program, the statement following the if-else statement is the next one to execute.

»NOTE
Do not include a semicolon at the end of the line containing the keyword if and the expression to be tested, or on the line with the keyword else. As you learned earlier, doing so is not a syntax error, but it can create a logic error in your program.

The following code sample illustrates an `if-else` statement written in C++:

```cpp
int hoursWorked = 45;
double rate = 15.00;
double grossPay;
string overtime = "Yes";
const int HOURS_IN_WEEK = 40;
const double OVERTIME_RATE = 1.5;
if (hoursWorked > HOURS_IN_WEEK)
{
    overtime = "Yes";
    grossPay = HOURS_IN_WEEK * rate + (hoursWorked - HOURS_IN_WEEK) *
        OVERTIME_RATE * rate;
}
else
{
    overtime = "No";
    grossPay = hoursWorked * rate;
}
cout << "Overtime: " << overtime << endl;
cout << "Gross Pay: $" << grossPay << endl;
```

▶▶ NOTE

HOURS_IN_WEEK is a constant that is initialized with the value 40 and OVERTIME_RATE is a constant that is initialized with the value 1.5.

In the preceding code, the value of the variable named `hoursWorked` is tested to see if it is greater than `HOURS_IN_WEEK`.

You use the greater than relational operator, >, to make the comparison. If the expression `hoursWorked > HOURS_IN_WEEK` evaluates to `true`, then the first block statement executes. This first block statement contains one statement that assigns the string constant `"Yes"` to the variable named `overtime`, and another statement that calculates the employee's gross pay, including overtime pay, and assigns the calculated value to the variable named `grossPay`.

If the expression `hoursWorked > HOURS_IN_WEEK`, evaluates to `false` then a different path is followed, and the second block statement following the keyword `else` executes. This block statement contains one statement that assigns the string constant `"No"` to the variable named `overtime`, and another statement that calculates the employee's gross pay with no overtime, and assigns the calculated value to the variable named `grossPay`.

Regardless of which path is taken in this code, the next statement to execute is the output statement `cout << "Overtime: " << overtime << endl;` immediately followed by the output statement `cout << "Gross Pay: $" << grossPay << endl;`.

EXERCISE 4-2: UNDERSTANDING IF-ELSE STATEMENTS

In this exercise, you use what you have learned about writing `if-else` statements in C++ to study a complete C++ program that uses `if-else` statements. This program was written to calculate customer charges for a telephone company. The telephone company charges 15 cents per minute for calls outside of the customer's area code that last over 20 minutes. All other calls are 20 cents per minute. Take a few minutes to study the code that follows, and then answer Questions 1 through 4.

```cpp
// Telephone.cpp - This program determines telephone call
// charges.
#include <iostream>
using namespace std;
int main()
{
    int custAC, custNumber;
    int calledAC, calledNumber;
    int callMinutes;
    double callCharge;
    const int MAX_MINS = 20;
    const double CHARGE_1 = .15;
    const double CHARGE_2 = .20;
    custAC = 630;
    custNumber = 5551234;
    calledAC = 219;
    calledNumber = 5557890;
    callMinutes = 35;
    if(calledAC != custAC && callMinutes > MAX_MINS)
        callCharge = callMinutes * CHARGE_1;
    else
        callCharge = callMinutes * CHARGE_2;
    cout << "Customer Number: " << custAC << "-" << custNumber
        << endl;
    cout << "Called Number: " << calledAC << "-" << calledNumber
        << endl;
    cout << "The charge for this call is $" << callCharge << endl;
    return 0;
}
```

1. What is the exact output when this program executes?

2. What is the exact output if the value of callMinutes is changed to 20?

3. What is the exact output if the expression in the if statement is changed to callMinutes >= MAX_MINS?

4. What is the exact output if the variable named `custAC` is assigned the value `312` rather than the value `630`?

_____

_____

_____

LAB 4-2: USING IF-ELSE STATEMENTS

In this lab, you complete a prewritten C++ program that computes the largest and smallest of three integer values. The three values are 210, 330, and –1.

1. Open the file named `LargeSmall.cpp` using Notepad or the text editor of your choice.

2. Two variables named `largest` and `smallest` are declared for you. Use these variables to store the largest and smallest of the three integer values. You must decide what other variables you will need and initialize them if appropriate.

3. Write the rest of the program using assignment statements, `if` statements, or `if-else` statements as appropriate. There are comments in the code that tell you where you should write your statements. The output statements are written for you.

4. Compile the program.

5. Execute the program. Your output should be:

```
The largest value is 330.
The smallest value is -1.
```

NESTED IF STATEMENTS

You can nest `if` statements to create a multipath decision statement. When you nest `if` statements, you include an `if` statement within another `if` statement. This is helpful in programs in which you want to provide more than two possible paths.

The syntax for writing a nested `if` statement in C++ is as follows:

```
if(expressionA)
    statementA;
else if(expressionB)
    statementB;
else
    statementC;
```

> **NOTE**
> Do not include a semicolon at the end of the lines with expressions to be tested or on the line with the keyword `else`.

This is called a nested `if` statement because the second `if` statement is a part of the first `if` statement. This is easier to see if the example is changed as follows:

```
if(expressionA)
    statementA;
else
    if(expressionB)
        statementB;
    else
        statementC;
```

Now let's see how a nested `if` statement works. If `expressionA`, which is enclosed in parentheses, evaluates to `true`, then the computer executes *statementA*. If `expressionA` evaluates to `false`, then the computer will evaluate `expressionB`. If `expressionB` evaluates to `true`, then the computer will execute *statementB*. If `expressionA` and `expressionB` both evaluate to `false`, then the computer will execute *statementC*. Regardless of which path is taken in this code, the statement following the `if-else` statement is the next one to execute.

The C++ code sample that follows illustrates a nested `if` statement.

```
if(empDept <= 3)
    supervisorName = "Dillon";
else if(empDept <= 7)
    supervisorName = "Escher";
else
    supervisorName = "Fontana";
cout << "Supervisor: " << supervisorName << endl;
```

When you read the preceding code, you can assume that a department number is never less than 1. If the value of the variable named `empDept` is less than or equal to the value 3 (in the range of values from 1 to 3), then the value `"Dillon"` is assigned to the variable named `supervisorName`. If the value of `empDept` is not less than or equal to 3, but it is less than or equal to 7 (in the range of values from 4 to 7), then the value `"Escher"` is assigned to the variable named `supervisorName`. If the value of `empDept` is not in the range of values from 1 to 7, then the value `"Fontana"` is assigned to the variable named `supervisorName`. As you can see, there are three possible paths this program could take when the nested `if` statement is encountered. Regardless of which path the program takes, the next statement to execute is the output statement `cout << "Supervisor: " << supervisorName << endl;`.

EXERCISE 4-3: UNDERSTANDING NESTED IF STATEMENTS

In this exercise, you use what you have learned about writing nested `if` statements in C++ to study a complete C++ program that uses nested `if` statements. This program was written for the Woof Wash dog-grooming business to calculate a total charge for services rendered. Woof Wash charges $30 for a bath, $20 for a cut, and $15 to clip nails. Take a few minutes to study the code that follows, and then answer Questions 1 through 3.

```
// WoofWash.cpp - This program determines if a doggy
// service is provided and prints the charge.
#include <iostream>
#include <string>
using namespace std;
int main()
{
```

```
        string service;
        const string SERVICE_1 = "bath";
        const string SERVICE_2 = "cut";
        const string SERVICE_3 = "trim nails";
        double charge;
        const double BATH_CHARGE = 30.00;
        const double CUT_CHARGE = 20.00;
        const double NAIL_CHARGE = 15.00;
        cout << "Enter service: ";
        cin >> service;
        if(service == SERVICE_1)
           charge = BATH_CHARGE;
        else if(service == SERVICE_2)
           charge = CUT_CHARGE;
        else if(service == SERVICE_3)
           charge = NAIL_CHARGE;
        else
           charge = 0.00;
        if(charge > 0.00)
           cout << "The charge for a doggy " << service << " is $"
               <<   charge << endl;
        else
           cout << "We do not perform the " << service << " service."
               << endl;
        return 0;
    }
```

1. What is the exact output when this program executes if the user enters "bath"?

_____

_____

2. What is the exact output when this program executes if the user enters "shave"?

_____

_____

3. What is the exact output when this program executes if the user enters "BATH"?

_____

_____

LAB 4-3: USING NESTED IF STATEMENTS

In this lab, you complete a prewritten C++ program that calculates an employee's end-of-year bonus and prints the employee's name, yearly salary, performance rating, and bonus. Bonuses are calculated based on an employee's annual salary and his or her performance rating. The rating system is contained in Table 4-4:

Rating	Bonus
1	10 percent of annual salary
2	6 percent of annual salary
3	3 percent of annual salary
4	None

Table 4-4 Employee ratings and bonuses

1. Open the file named `EmployeeBonus.cpp` using Notepad or the text editor of your choice.

2. Variables have been declared for you and the input statements and output statements have been written. Read them over carefully before you proceed to the next step.

3. Design the logic and write the rest of the program using a nested `if` statement.

4. Compile the program.

5. Execute the program and enter the following as input:

   Employee's first name - **Laurie**

   Employee's last name - **Blair**

   Employee's salary - **65000.00**

   Employee's performance rating - **3**

6. Your output should be:

   ```
   Employee Name: Laurie Blair
   Employee Salary: $65000
   Employee Rating: 3
   Employee Bonus: $1950
   ```

Note: You cannot control the number of places that appear after the decimal point until you learn more about C++ in Chapter 7 of this book.

THE SWITCH STATEMENT

The `switch` statement is similar to a nested `if` statement because it is also a multipath decision statement. A `switch` statement offers the advantage of being easier for you to read than nested `if` statements, and a `switch` statement is also easier for you, the programmer, to maintain. You use the `switch` statement in situations when you want to compare an expression with several integer constants.

The syntax for writing a `switch` statement in C++ is as follows:

```
switch (expression)
{
    case constant: statement(s);
    case constant: statement(s);
    case constant: statement(s);
    default:       statement(s);
}
```

NOTE
If you omit a
break statement
in a case, all the
code up to the next
break statement
or a closing curly
brace is executed.
This is probably not
what you intend.

You begin writing a `switch` statement with the keyword `switch`. Then, within parentheses, you include an expression that evaluates to an integer value. Cases are then defined within the `switch` statement by using the keyword `case` as a label, and including an integer value after this label. For example, you could include an integer constant such as 10 or an arithmetic expression that evaluates to an integer such as 10/2. The computer evaluates the expression in the `switch` statement and then compares it to the integer values following the `case` labels. If the expression and the integer value match, then the computer executes the statement(s) that follow until it encounters a `break` statement or a closing curly brace. The `break` statement causes an exit from the `switch` statement. You can use the keyword `default` to establish a case for values that do not match any of the integer values following the `case` labels. Note also that all of the cases, including the default case, are enclosed within curly braces.

The following code sample illustrates the use of the `switch` statement in C++:

```cpp
int deptNum;
string deptName;
deptNum = 2;
switch (deptNum)
{
    case 1:     deptName = "Marketing";
                break;
    case 2:     deptName = "Development";
                break;
    case 3:     deptName = "Sales";
                break;
    default:    deptName = "Unknown";
                break;
}
cout << "Department: " << deptName << endl;
```

In the preceding example, when the program encounters the `switch` statement, the value of the variable named `deptNum` is 2. The value 2 matches the integer constant 2 in the second case of the `switch` statement. Therefore, the string constant `"Development"` is assigned to the `string` object named `deptName`. A `break` statement is encountered next, and causes the program to exit from the `switch` statement. The statement following the switch statement `cout << "Department: " << deptName << endl;` executes next.

If the `break` statements in the preceding example were omitted and the value of `deptNum` was 2, all of the statements up to the closing curly brace would execute. The output would be: `Department: Unknown`. In this example, omitting the `break` statements would be considered a logic error.

EXERCISE 4-4: USING A `SWITCH` STATEMENT

In this exercise, you use what you have learned about the `switch` statement to study some C++ code, and then answer the questions that follow.

First, examine the following code:

```
int numValue = 2;
int answer = 0;
switch(numValue)
{
    case 1:   answer += 1;
    case 2:   answer += 2;
    case 3:   answer += 3;
              break;
    case 4:   answer += 4;
    case 5:   answer += 5;
    default:  answer = 0;
              break;
}
cout << "Answer: " << answer << endl;
```

1. What is the value of `answer` if the value of `numValue` is 2?

   _____

2. What is the value of `answer` if the value of `numValue` is 4?

   _____

3. What is the value of `answer` if the value of `numValue` is 1?

   _____

4. What is the value of `answer` if the value of `numValue` is 22?

   _____

5. Is the `break` statement in the `default` case needed? Explain.

   _____

LAB 4-4: USING A `SWITCH` STATEMENT

In this lab, you complete a prewritten C++ program that calculates an employee's end-of-year bonus and prints the employee's name, yearly salary, performance rating, and bonus. This is the same program you wrote in Lab 4-3 when you used nested `if` statements to write the program. This time you use a `switch` statement instead of nested `if` statements.

In this program, bonuses are calculated based on employees' annual salary and their performance rating. The rating system is contained in Table 4-5:

Rating	Bonus
1	10 percent of annual salary
2	6 percent of annual salary
3	3 percent of annual salary
4	None

Table 4-5 Employee ratings and bonuses

1. Open the file named `EmployeeBonus2.cpp` using Notepad or the text editor of your choice.

2. Variables have been declared for you and the input statements and output statements have been written. Read them over carefully before you proceed to the next step.

3. Design the logic and write the rest of the program using a `switch` statement.

4. Compile the program.

5. Execute the program entering the following as input:

   Employee's name - **Laurie Blair**

   Employee's salary - **65000.00**

   Employee's performance rating – **3**

6. Confirm that your output matches the following:

```
Employee Name: Laurie Blair
Employee Salary: $65000
Employee Rating: 3
Employee Bonus: $1950
```

USING DECISION STATEMENTS TO MAKE MULTIPLE COMPARISONS

When you write programs, you must often write statements that include multiple comparisons. For example, you may want to determine that two conditions are `true` before you decide which path your program will take. In the next sections, you learn how to implement AND logic in a program by using the `&&` (AND) logical operator. You also learn how to implement OR logic using the `||` (OR) logical operator.

USING AND LOGIC

When you write C++ programs, you can use the AND operator (&&) to make multiple comparisons in a single decision statement. Remember when using AND logic that all expressions must evaluate to `true` for the entire expression to be `true`.

The C++ code that follows illustrates a decision statement that uses the AND operator (&&) to implement AND logic:

```
string medicalPlan = "Y";
string dentalPlan = "Y";
if((medicalPlan == "Y") && (dentalPlan == "Y"))
    cout << "Employee has medical insurance" <<
            " and also has dental insurance." << endl;
else
    cout << "Employee may have medical insurance or may " <<
            "have dental insurance, but does not have both " <<
            "medical and dental insurance." << endl;
```

In this example, the variables named `medicalPlan` and `dentalPlan` have both been initialized to the string constant "Y". When the expression `medicalPlan == "Y"` is evaluated, the result is `true`. When the expression `dentalPlan == "Y"` is evaluated, the result is also `true`. Because both expressions evaluate to `true`, the entire expression `medicalPlan == "Y" && dentalPlan == "Y"` evaluates to `true`. Because the entire expression is `true`, the output generated is "Employee has medical insurance and also has dental insurance."

If you initialize either of the variables `medicalPlan` or `dentalPlan` with a value other than "Y", then the expression `medicalPlan == "Y" && dentalPlan == "Y"` evaluates to `false`, and the output generated is "Employee may have medical insurance or may have dental insurance, but does not have both medical and dental insurance."

USING OR LOGIC

You can use OR logic when you want to make multiple comparisons in a single decision statement. Of course, you must remember when using OR logic that only one expression must evaluate to `true` for the entire expression to be `true`.

The C++ code that follows illustrates a decision statement that uses the OR operator (||) to implement OR logic:

```
string medicalPlan = "Y";
string dentalPlan = "N";
if(medicalPlan == "Y" || dentalPlan == "Y")
    cout << "Employee has medical insurance or dental " <<
            "insurance or both." << endl;
else
    cout << "Employee does not have medical insurance " <<
            "and also does not have dental insurance." << endl;
```

In this example, the variable named medicalPlan is initialized with the string constant "Y", and the variable named dentalPlan is initialized to the string constant "N". When the expression medicalPlan == "Y" is evaluated, the result is true. When the expression dentalPlan == "Y" is evaluated, the result is false. The expression medicalPlan == "Y" || dentalPlan == "Y" evaluates to true because when using OR logic, only one of the expressions must evaluate to true for the entire expression to be true. Because the entire expression is true, the output generated is "Employee has medical insurance or dental insurance or both."

If you initialize both of the variables medicalPlan and dentalPlan with the string constant "N", then the expression medicalPlan == "Y" || dentalPlan == "Y" evaluates to false, and the output generated is "Employee does not have medical insurance and also does not have dental insurance."

EXERCISE 4-5: MAKING MULTIPLE COMPARISONS IN DECISION STATEMENTS

In this exercise, you use what you have learned about OR logic to study a complete C++ program that uses OR logic in a decision statement. This program was written for a marketing research firm that wants to determine if a customer prefers Coke or Pepsi over some other drink. Take a few minutes to study the code that follows, and then answer Questions 1 through 4.

```cpp
// CokeOrPepsi.cpp - This program determines if a customer prefers to
// drink Coke or Pepsi or some other drink.
#include <iostream>
#include <string>
using namespace std;
int main()
{
    string customerFirstName;    // Customer's first name
    string customerLastName;     // Customer's last name
    string drink = "";           // Customer's favorite drink

    cout << "Enter customer's first name: ";
    cin >> customerFirstName;
    cout << "Enter customer's last name: ";
    cin >> customerLastName;
    cout << "Enter customer's drink preference: ";
    cin >> drink;

    if(drink == "Coke" || drink == "Pepsi")
    {
        cout << "Customer First Name: " << customerFirstName << endl;
        cout << "Customer Last Name: " << customerLastName << endl;
        cout << "Drink: " << drink << endl;
    }
    else
        cout << customerFirstName << " " << customerLastName
             << " does not prefer Coke or Pepsi." << endl;
    return 0;
}
```

1. What is the exact output when this program executes if the customer's name is Sally Preston and the drink is Coke?

   _____

   _____

2. What is the exact output when this program executes if the customer's name is Sally Preston and the drink is Pepsi?

   _____

   _____

3. What is the exact output from this program when

   ```
   if(drink == "Coke" || drink == "Pepsi")
   ```

   is changed to

   ```
   if(drink == "Coke" && drink == "Pepsi")
   ```

   and the customer's name is Sally Preston and the drink is Coke?

   _____

   _____

4. What is the exact output from this program when

   ```
   if(drink == "Coke" || drink == "Pepsi")
   ```

   is changed to

   ```
   if(drink == "Coke" || drink == "Pepsi" || drink == "coke" ||
   drink == "pepsi")
   ```

   and the customer's name is Sally Preston, and the drink is pepsi? What does this change allow a user to enter?

   _____

   _____

LAB 4-5: MAKING MULTIPLE COMPARISONS IN DECISION STATEMENTS

In this lab, you complete a partially written C++ program for an airline that offers a 15% discount to passengers who are 12 years old or younger and the same discount to passengers who are 65 years old or older. The program should request a passenger's name and age and then print whether the passenger is eligible or not eligible for a discount.

1. Open the file named `Airline.cpp` using Notepad or the text editor of your choice.

2. Variables have been declared and initialized for you, and the input statements have been written. Read them carefully before you proceed to the next step.

3. Design the logic deciding whether to use AND or OR logic. Write the decision statement to identify when a discount should be offered and when a discount should not be offered.

4. Be sure to include output statements telling whether or not the customer is eligible for a discount.

5. Compile the program.

6. Execute the program, entering the following as input:

   a. Customer Name - Connie Chen

      Customer Age - 22

      What is the output? _____

   b. Customer Name - William Gorman

      Customer Age - 65

      What is the output? _____

   c. Customer Name - Maria Gonzales

      Customer Age - 72

      What is the output? _____

   d. Customer Name - Sheila Morton

      Customer Age - 52

      What is the output? _____

   e. Customer Name - Timmy Morton

      Customer Age - 2

      What is the output? _____

   f. Customer Name - Helen Patel

      Customer Age - 12

      What is the output? _____

5

WRITING PROGRAMS USING LOOPS

After studying this chapter, you will be able to:

Use C++ increment (++) and decrement (--) operators
Recognize how and when to use `while` loops in C++,
    including how to use a counter and how to use
    a sentinel value to control a loop
Use `for` loops in C++
Write a `do-while` loop in C++
Include nested loops in applications
Accumulate totals by using a loop in a C++ application
Use a loop to validate user input in an application

In this chapter, you learn how to use C++ to program three types of loops: a `while` loop, a `do-while` loop, and a `for` loop. You also learn how to nest loops, how to use a loop to help you accumulate a total in your programs, and how to use a loop to validate user input. But before you get started with learning about C++'s loops, it is helpful to learn about two additional operators: the increment and decrement operators.

You should do the exercises and labs in this chapter after you have finished Chapter 5 in your book, *Programming Logic and Design, Fifth Edition*, by Joyce Farrell. In that chapter, you learned that loops change the flow of control in a program by allowing a programmer to direct the computer to execute a statement or a group of statements multiple times.

THE INCREMENT (++) AND DECREMENT (––) OPERATORS

▶▶NOTE
The "l" in "lvalue" represents "left."

You often use the increment and decrement operators when your programs require loops. These operators provide a concise, efficient method for adding 1 to (incrementing) or subtracting 1 from (decrementing) an lvalue. An **lvalue** is an area of memory in which a value that your program needs may be stored. In C++ code, you place an lvalue on the left side of an assignment statement. Recall that an assignment statement stores a value at a memory location that is associated with a variable, and you place a variable name on the left side of an assignment statement.

▶▶NOTE
The increment and decrement operators may be used only with integer data types.

For example, the C++ assignment statement.

```
number = 10;
```

assigns the value 10 to the variable named `number`. This causes the computer to store the value 10 at the memory location associated with `number`. Because the increment and decrement operators add 1 to or subtract 1 from an lvalue, the statement `number++;` is equivalent to `number = number + 1;` and the statement `number--;` is equivalent to `number = number - 1;`. Each expression in these statements changes or writes to the memory location associated with the variable named `number`.

Both the increment and decrement operators have prefix and postfix forms. Which form you use depends on when you want to increment or decrement the value stored in the variable. When you use the **prefix form**, as in `++number`, you place the operator in front of the name of the variable. This increments or decrements the lvalue immediately. When you use the **postfix form**, as in `number++`, you place the operator after the name of the variable. This increments or decrements the lvalue after it is used.

The example that follows illustrates the use of both forms of the increment operator in C++:

```
x = 5;
y = x++;   // Postfix form
           // y is assigned the value of x,
           // then x is incremented.
           // Value of y is 5.
           // Value of x is 6.
```

```
x = 5;
y = ++x;   // Prefix form
           // x is incremented first, then
           // the value of x is assigned to y.
           // Value of y is 6.
           // Value of x is 6.
```

You might understand the postfix form better if you think of the statement y = x++; as being the same as the following:

```
x = 5;
y = x;
x = x + 1;
```

To understand the prefix form better, think of y = ++x; as being the same as the following:

```
x = 5;
x = x + 1;
y = x;
```

EXERCISE 5-1: USING THE INCREMENT AND DECREMENT OPERATORS

In this exercise, you examine the code and use what you have learned about C++'s increment and decrement operators to answer the related questions.

1. Examine the following code:

   ```
   x = 7;

   y = ++x;
   ```

   After this code executes, what is the value of x? _____ y? _____

2. Examine the following code:

   ```
   x = 7;

   y = x++;
   ```

   After this code executes, what is the value of x? _____ y? _____

3. Examine the following code:

   ```
   x = 7;

   y = --x;
   ```

   After this code executes, what is the value of x? _____ y? _____

4. Examine the following code:

   ```
   x = 7;

   y = x--;
   ```

   After this code executes, what is the value of x? _____ y? _____

WRITING A WHILE LOOP IN C++

As you learned in *Programming Logic and Design, Fifth Edition*, three steps must occur in every loop:

1. You must initialize a variable that will control the loop. This variable is known as the **loop control variable**.

2. You must compare the loop control variable to some value, known as the **sentinel value**, which decides whether the loop continues or stops. This decision is based on a Boolean comparison. The result of a **Boolean** comparison is always a `true` or `false` value.

3. Within the loop, you must alter the value of the loop control variable.

You also learned that the statements that are part of a loop are referred to as the **loop body**. In C++, the loop body may consist of a single statement or a block statement.

>> **NOTE**
Remember that a block statement is several statements within a pair of curly braces.

The statements that make up a loop body may be any type of statement, including assignment statements, decision statements, or even other loops. Note that the C++ syntax for writing a `while` loop is as follows:

```
while(expression)
    statement;
```

Notice that there is no semicolon after the ending parenthesis. Placing a semicolon after the ending parenthesis is not a syntax error, but it is a logic error. It results in an **infinite loop**, which is a loop that never stops executing the statements in its body. It never stops executing because the semicolon is a statement called the null statement and is interpreted as "do nothing." Think of a `while` loop with a semicolon after the ending parenthesis as meaning "while the condition is true, do nothing forever."

The `while` loop allows you to direct the computer to execute the statement in the body of the loop as long as the expression within the parentheses evaluates to `true`. Study the example that follows, which illustrates a `while` loop that uses a block statement as its loop body:

```
const int NUM_TIMES = 3;
num = 0;
while(num < NUM_TIMES)
{
    cout << "Welcome to C++ Programming." << endl;
    num++;
}
```

In the preceding example, a block statement is used because the loop body contains more than one statement.

The first statement in the loop body causes the text "Welcome to C++ Programming." to appear on the user's screen. The second statement, num++, is important because it causes num, the loop control variable, to be incremented. When the loop is first encountered, the comparison `num < NUM_TIMES` is made for the first time when the value of `num` is 0. The 0 is compared to, and found to be less than, 3, which means the condition is `true`, and the text "Welcome to C++ Programming." is displayed for the first time. The next statement, `num++;`, causes 1 to be added to the value of `num`. The second time the comparison is made, the value of `num` is 1, which is still less than 3, and causes the text to appear a second time followed by adding 1 to the value of `num`. The third comparison also results in a `true` value because the value of `num` is now 2, and 2 is still less than 3; as a result, the text appears a third time and `num` is incremented again. The fourth time the comparison is made, the value of `num` is 3, which is not less than 3; as a result, the program exits the loop.

The loop in the next code example produces the same results as the previous example. The text "Welcome to C++ Programming." is displayed three times.

```cpp
const int NUM_TIMES = 3;
num = 0;
while(num++ < NUM_TIMES)
    cout << "Welcome to C++ Programming." << endl;
```

Be sure you understand why the postfix increment operator is used in the expression `num++ < NUM_TIMES`.

The first time this comparison is made, the value of `num` is 0. The 0 is then compared to, and found to be less than, 3, which means the condition is `true`, and the text "Welcome to C++ Programming." is displayed.

The second time the comparison is made, the value of `num` is 1, which is still less than 3, which causes the text to appear a second time. The third comparison also results in a `true` value because the value of `num` is now 2, and 2 is still less than 3; as a result, the text appears a third time. The fourth time the comparison is made, the value of `num` is 3, which is not less than 3; as a result, the program exits the loop.

If the prefix increment operator is used in the expression `++num < NUM_TIMES`, the loop executes twice instead of three times. The loop executes twice because the first time this comparison is made, `num` is incremented before the comparison is done. This results in `num` having a value of 1 the first time "Welcome to C++ Programming." is displayed and a value of 2 the second time it is displayed. Then, when the value of `num` is 3, the condition is `false`, causing the program to exit the loop. This time, "Welcome to C++ Programming." is not displayed.

»NOTE
When you use the postfix increment operator, the value of `num` is not incremented until after the comparison is made.

»NOTE
Failing to learn the difference between the prefix and postfix forms of the increment and decrement operators can result in serious program errors.

EXERCISE 5-2: USING A WHILE LOOP

In this exercise, you use what you have learned about writing `while` loops to study the following code and then answer the subsequent questions.

First, study the C++ code:

```cpp
const int NUM_LOOPS = 5;
int numTimes = NUM_LOOPS;
while(numTimes++ < NUM_LOOPS)
    cout << "Value of numTimes is " << numTimes << endl;
```

1. What is the loop control variable? What is the sentinel value?

   _____

   _____

2. What is the output?

   _____

3. What is the output if the code is changed to `while(numTimes++ <= NUM_LOOPS)`?

   _____

4. What is the output if the code is changed to `while(++numTimes <= NUM_LOOPS)`?

   _____

USING A COUNTER TO CONTROL A LOOP

In Chapter 5 of *Programming Logic and Design, Fifth Edition*, you learned that you can use a counter to control a `while` loop. With a counter, you set up the loop to execute a specified number of times. Also recall that a `while` loop may execute zero times if the expression used in the comparison immediately evaluates to `false`. In that case, the computer does not execute the body of the loop at all.

Chapter 5 of *Programming Logic and Design, Fifth Edition* discusses a counter-controlled loop that controls how many times the word "Hello" is printed. Let's take a look at the following pseudocode for this counter-controlled loop:

```
num count = 0
while count < 4
    print "Hello"
    count = count + 1
endwhile
```

The counter for this loop is a variable named `count`, which is assigned the value 0 and the sentinel value is 4. The Boolean expression `count < 4` is tested to see if the value of `count` is less than 4. If `true`, the loop executes. If `false`, the program exits the loop. If the loop executes, the program displays the word "Hello", and then adds 1 to the value of `count`. Given this pseudocode, the loop body executes four times and the word "Hello" is displayed four times.

Now, let's see what the code looks like when you translate the pseudocode to C++:

```
int count = 0;
while(count < 4)
{
    cout << "Hello" << endl;
    count++;
}
```

First, the variable `count` is assigned a value of 0 and is used as the counter variable to control the `while` loop. The `while` loop follows and includes the Boolean expression `count < 4` within parentheses. The counter-controlled loop executes a block statement that is marked by an opening curly brace and a closing curly brace. The statements in the loop body display the word "Hello" and then increment count, which adds 1 to the counter variable.

> **NOTE**
> Incrementing the counter variable is an important statement. Each time through the loop, the count variable must be incremented or the expression count < 4 would never be false. This would result in an infinite loop.

EXERCISE 5-3: USING A COUNTER-CONTROLLED WHILE LOOP

In this exercise, you use what you have learned about counter-controlled loops to answer questions about the following code:

```
number1 = 0;
number2 = 0;
while(number1 < 5)
    number1++;
    number2 += number1;
```

1. What is the value of number1 when the loop exits? _____

2. What is the value of number2 when the loop exits? _____

3. If the statement number1++ is changed to ++number1, what is the value of number1 when the loop exits? _____

4. What could you do to force the value of number2 to be 15 when the loop exits?
_____

LAB 5-1: USING A COUNTER-CONTROLLED WHILE LOOP

In this lab, you use a counter-controlled while loop in a C++ program provided with the data files for this book. When completed, the program should print the numbers 0 through 10, along with their values doubled and tripled. The data file contains the necessary variable declarations and output statements.

> **NOTE**
> Remember that number2 += number1; is the same as number2 = number2 + number1;.

1. Open the source code file named DoubleTriple.cpp using Notepad or the text editor of your choice.

2. Write a counter-controlled while loop that uses the loop control variable to take on the values 0 through 10. Remember to initialize the loop control variable before the program enters the loop.

3. In the body of the loop, calculate the double and the triple using the value of the loop control variable. Remember to change the value of the loop control variable in the body of the loop.

4. Save the source code file in a directory of your choice and then make that directory your working directory.

5. Compile the source code file DoubleTriple.cpp.

6. Execute the program.

_____
_____

USING A SENTINEL VALUE TO CONTROL A LOOP

As you learned in Chapter 2 of *Programming Logic and Design, Fifth Edition*, a **sentinel value** is a value such as "Y" or "N" that a user must supply to stop a loop. To learn about sentinel values in C++, we will look at a program discussed in Chapter 5 of *Programming Logic and Design, Fifth Edition*. The program displays a bank customer's current bank balance, and then asks if the user wants to calculate the customer's balance after one year of interest has accumulated. Each time the user indicates he or she wants to continue, an increased balance appears. When the user indicates he or she is done, the program ends. This program includes a `while` loop and uses a sentinel value to determine when the loop executes or when the loop is exited. The pseudocode is shown below:

```
start
    num bankBal
    num intRate
    string response
    print "Enter your starting balance... "
    get bankBal
    print "Enter your interest rate... "
    get intRate
    print "Do you want to see your current balance? Y or N . . ."
    get response
    while response = 'Y'
        print "Bank balance is ", bankBal
        bankBal = bankBal + bankBal * intRate
        print "Do you want to see next year's balance? Y or N . . .")
        get response
    endwhile
    print "Have a nice day!"
stop
```

Note that a priming read is included in the pseudocode. Recall that you perform a **priming read** before a loop executes to input a value that is then used to control the loop. When a priming read is used, remember that you must perform another read within the loop body to get the next input value. You can see the priming read, the loop, and the last output statement portion of the pseudocode translated to C++ in the following code sample:

```cpp
cout << "Do you want to see your current balance? Y or N: ";
cin >> response;
while(response == "Y")
{
    cout << "Bank balance is " << bankBal << endl;
    bankBal = bankBal + bankBal * intRate;
    cout << "Do you want to see next year's balance? Y or N: ";
    cin >> response;
}
cout << "Have a nice day!" << endl;
```

In this code example, the variable named `response` is the loop control variable. It is assigned a value when the program asks the user, "Do you want to see your current balance? Y or N:"

and reads the user's response. The loop control variable is tested with `response == "Y"`. If the user enters `Y`, which is the sentinel value, then the test expression is `true` and the four statements within the loop body execute.

The first statement displays the value of `bankBal`. Next, the value of `bankBal` is recalculated using the value of `intRate`, the third statement prompts the user for a new value for `response`, and the fourth statement retrieves the user's input and stores it in `response`. This is the statement that may change the value of the loop control variable. The loop body ends when program control returns to the top of the loop, where the Boolean expression in the `while` statement is tested again. If the user entered `Y` at the last prompt, then the loop is entered again and the new value of `bankBal` is displayed. If the user enters any response other than `Y`, then the test expression is `false`, and the loop body doesn't execute. When the loop is exited, the next statement to execute displays "Have a nice day!"

EXERCISE 5-4: USING A SENTINEL VALUE TO CONTROL A `WHILE` LOOP

In this exercise, you use what you have learned about sentinel values to answer questions about the following code:

```
cout << "How many pages do you want to print? ";
cin >> numToPrint;
counter = 1;
while(counter <= numToPrint);
{
    cout << "Page Number " << counter << endl;
    counter++;
}
cout << "Value of counter is " << counter << endl;
```

1. What is the output if the user enters a 5?

   _____

2. What is the problem with this code and how can you fix it?

   _____

3. Assuming you fix the problem, if the user enters 200 as the number of pages to print, what is the value of `counter` when the loop exits?

   _____

4. Assuming you fix the problem, if the user enters 21 as the number of pages to print, how many pages will print?

   _____

5. What is the output if the curly braces are deleted?

   _____

LAB 5-2: USING A SENTINEL VALUE TO CONTROL A WHILE LOOP

In this lab, you write a while loop that uses a sentinel value to control a loop in a C++ program provided with the data files for this book. You also write the statements that make up the body of the loop. The source code file already contains the necessary variable declarations and output statements. When completed, the program should print a payoff schedule for a credit card company customer. At the beginning of every month, 1.3% interest is added to the balance, and then the customer makes a payment equal to 4% of the current balance. When the balance reaches $15.00 or less, the customer can pay off the account. As you will see, this program generates a lot of output, even for one customer.

1. Open the source code file named Payoff.cpp using Notepad or the text editor of your choice.

2. Write the while loop using a sentinel value to control the loop and also write the statements that make up the body of the loop. The output statements within the loop have already been written for you.

3. Save this source code file in a directory of your choice and then make that directory your working directory.

4. Compile the source code file Payoff.cpp.

5. Execute the program. Input the following:

   Account Number: 6789A

   Customer Name: Jeanne Johnson

   Balance: 120.00

6. Record the final balance amount when the loan may be paid off.

WRITING A FOR LOOP IN C++

In Chapter 5 of *Programming Logic and Design, Fifth Edition,* you learned that a for loop is a **definite** loop; this means this type of loop will execute a definite number of times. The following is the syntax for a for loop in C++:

```
for(expression1; expression2; expression3)
     statement;
```

In C++, the `for` loop consists of three expressions that are separated by semicolons and enclosed within parentheses. The `for` loop executes as follows:

» The first time the `for` loop is encountered, the first expression is evaluated. Usually, this expression initializes a variable that is used to control the `for` loop.

» Next, the second expression is evaluated. The second expression usually evaluates the variable that was initialized in the first expression. If the second expression evaluates to `true`, the loop statement executes. If the second expression evaluates to `false`, the loop is exited.

» After the loop statement executes, the third expression is evaluated. The third expression usually increments or decrements the variable that you initialized in the first expression and compared in the second expression.

» After the third expression is evaluated, the second expression is evaluated again. If the second expression still evaluates to `true`, the loop statement executes again, and then the third expression is evaluated again. This process continues until the second expression evaluates to `false`.

The following code sample illustrates a C++ `for` loop. Notice that the code uses a block statement in the `for` loop.

```cpp
int number = 0;
int count;
const int NUM_LOOPS = 10;
for(count = 0; count < NUM_LOOPS; count++)
{
    number += count;
    cout << "Value of number is: " << number << endl;
}
```

In this `for` loop example, the variable named `count` is initialized to `0` in the first expression. The second expression is a Boolean expression that evaluates to `true` or `false`. When the expression `count < NUM_LOOPS` is evaluated the first time, the value of `count` is `0` and the result is `true`. The loop body is then entered. This is where a new value is computed and assigned to the variable named `number` and then is displayed. The first time through the loop, the output is as follows: `Value of number is: 0`.

After the output is displayed, the third expression in the `for` loop is evaluated; this adds `1` to the value of `count`, making the new value of `count` equal to `1`. When expression two is evaluated a second time, the value of `count` is `1`. The program then tests to see if the value of `count` is less than `NUM_LOOPS`. This results in a `true` value and causes the loop body to execute again where a new value is computed for `number` and then displayed. The second time through the loop, the output is as follows: `Value of number is: 1`.

Next, expression three is evaluated; this adds `1` to the value of `count`. The value of `count` is now `2`. Expression two is evaluated a third time and again is `true` because `2` is less than `NUM_LOOPS`. The third time through, the loop body changes the value of `number` to `3` and then displays the new value. The output is as follows: `Value of number is: 3`.

This process continues until the value of count becomes 10. At this time, 10 is not less than NUM_LOOPS, so the second expression results in a false value, and causes an exit from the for loop.

The counter-controlled loop that displays the word "Hello" four times (explained in the "Using a Counter to Control a Loop" section of this chapter) can be rewritten using a for loop instead of the while loop. In fact, when you know how many times a loop will execute, it is considered a good programming practice to use a for loop instead of a while loop.

To rewrite the while loop as a for loop, you can change the statement int counter = 0; to int counter; because you initialize counter with the value 0 in expression one. You can also delete counter++; from the loop body because you increment counter in expression three. You continue to print the word "Hello" in the body of the loop. The following code sample illustrates this for loop:

```
int counter;
for(counter = 0; counter < 4; counter++)
{
    cout << "Hello" << endl;
}
```

> **»NOTE** The curly braces are not required because now the loop body contains just one statement. However, it is considered a good programming practice to include them, as it makes the code more readable and may help prevent an error later if additional statements are added to the body of the loop.

EXERCISE 5-5: USING A FOR LOOP

In this exercise, you use what you have learned about for loops to answer questions about the following code:

```
const int NUM_LOOPS = 18;
int numTimes;
for(numTimes = 1; numTimes <= NUM_LOOPS; numTimes++)
{
    cout << "Value of numTimes is: " << numTimes << endl;
    numTimes++;
}
```

Answer the following four questions by writing True or False:

1. This loop executes 18 times. _____

2. This loop could be written as a while loop. _____

3. Changing the <= operator to < will make no difference in the output. _____

4. This loop executes nine times. _____

LAB 5-3: USING A FOR LOOP

In this lab, you work with the same C++ program you worked with in Lab 5-1. As in Lab 5-1, the completed program should print the numbers 0 through 10, along with their values doubled and tripled. However, in this lab you should accomplish this using a for loop instead of a counter-controlled while loop.

1. Open the source code file named NewDoubleTriple.cpp using Notepad or the text editor of your choice.

2. Write a for loop that uses the loop control variable to take on the values 0 through 10.

3. In the body of the loop, calculate the double and the triple using the value of the loop control variable.

4. Save this source code file in a directory of your choice, and then make that directory your working directory.

5. Compile the source code file NewDoubleTriple.cpp.

6. Execute the program. Is the output the same?

WRITING A DO-WHILE LOOP IN C++

In Chapter 5 of *Programming Logic and Design, Fifth Edition*, you learned about the do-until loop. C++ does not support a do-until loop, but it does have a do-while loop. The do-while loop uses logic that can be stated as "do a while b is true." This is the same as a while loop, except that the condition is tested after the do-while loop body executes once. As a result, you should choose a do-while loop when your program logic requires the body of the loop to execute at least once. The body of a do-while loop continues to execute as long as the expression evaluates to true. The do-while syntax is as follows:

```
do
    statement;
while (expression);
```

The following do-while loop is a revised version of the while loop you saw earlier, which prints the word "Hello" four times. In this version, the loop is rewritten as a do-while loop.

```
counter = 0;
do
{
    cout << "Hello" << endl;
    counter++;
} while (counter < 4);
```

In this example, notice that you use block statements in do-while loops just as in while and for loops. When this loop is entered, the word "Hello" is printed, the value of counter is incremented, and then the value of counter is compared with the value 4. Notice that the word "Hello" will always be printed at least once because the loop control variable, counter, is compared to the value 4 at the bottom of the loop.

EXERCISE 5-6: USING A DO-WHILE LOOP

In this exercise, you use what you have learned about do-while loops to answer questions about the following code:

```
const int NUM_TIMES = 4;
int loopNum = 0;
do
{
    loopNum++;
    cout << "Ball " << loopNum << endl;
}while(loopNum < NUM_TIMES);
```

1. How many times does this loop execute? _____

2. What is the output of this program?

   _____

   _____

   _____

   _____

3. Is the output different if you change the order of the statements in the body of the loop, so that loopNum++ comes after the output statement?_____

4. What is the loop control variable?

   _____

LAB 5-4: USING A DO-WHILE LOOP

In this lab, you work with the same C++ program you worked with in Labs 5-1 and 5-3. As in those earlier labs, the completed program should print the numbers 0 through 10, along with their values doubled and tripled. However, in this lab you should accomplish this using a do-while loop.

By revising the same file three different ways in this chapter, you have seen that a single problem can be solved in different ways.

1. Open the source code file named NewestDoubleTriple.cpp using Notepad or the text editor of your choice.

2. Write a `do-while` loop that uses the loop control variable to take on the values 0 through 10.

3. In the body of the loop, calculate the double and the triple using the value of the loop control variable.

4. Save this source code file in a directory of your choice and then make that directory your working directory.

5. Compile the source code file `NewestDoubleTriple.cpp`.

6. Execute the program. Is the output the same?

NESTING LOOPS

As the logic of your programs becomes more complex, you may find that you need to use nested loops. That is, you may need to include a loop within another loop. You have learned that when you use nested loops in a program, you must use multiple control variables to control the separate loops.

In *Programming Logic and Design, Fifth Edition*, you studied the design logic for a program that produces a variable number of labels for every employee. A section of the pseudocode for this program is as follows:

```
print "Enter employee's name or " + QUIT + " to quit... "
get name
while name not equal to QUIT
    print "Enter number of units produced... "
    get production
    labelCounter = 0
    while labelCounter not equal to production
        print LABEL_TEXT, name
        labelCounter = labelCounter + 1
    endwhile
    print "Next name or " + QUIT + " to quit..."
    get name
endwhile
```

This pseudocode includes two loops. The outer loop uses the loop control variable `name` to control the loop using a sentinel value. The inner loop uses the control variable `labelCounter` to keep track of the number of labels to print for an employee. Refer to Chapter 5 in *Programming Logic and Design, Fifth Edition* for a line-by-line description of the pseudocode. When you are sure you understand the logic, take a look at the code sample that follows. This code sample shows the C++ code for the label printing program.

```cpp
// EmployeeLabels.cpp - This program prints a variable number of
// labels for individual employees.
#include <iostream>
#include <string>
using namespace std;
int main()
{
    string name;
    int production;
    int labelCounter;
    const string LABEL_TEXT = "Made for you personally by ";
    const string QUIT = "ZZZ";

    cout << "Enter employee's name or " << QUIT << " to quit.   ";
    cin >> name;
    while(name != QUIT)
    {
        cout << "Enter number of units produced: ";
        cin >> production;
        labelCounter = 0;
        while(labelCounter != production)
        {
            cout << LABEL_TEXT <<   name << endl;
            labelCounter++;
        }
        cout << "Next name or " << QUIT << " to quit.   ";
        cin >> name;
    }
    return 0;
}
```

This C++ program is saved in a file named EmployeeLabels.cpp and is included with the data files for this book. You may want to study the source code, compile it, and execute the program to experience how nested loops behave. The output from this program with Dan, Karen, and Ed entered as employee names and 3, 5, and 2 entered as the number of units produced is displayed in Figure 5-1.

Figure 5-1 Output generated by EmployeeLabels.cpp

EXERCISE 5-7: NESTING LOOPS

In this exercise, you use what you have learned about nesting loops in C++ to answer questions about the following code:

```
int sum = 0;
const int MAX_ROWS = 6, MAX_COLS = 3;
int rows, columns;
for(rows = 0; rows < MAX_ROWS; rows++)
    for(columns = 0; columns < MAX_COLS; columns++)
        sum += rows + columns;
cout << "Value of sum is " << sum << endl;
```

1. How many times does the outer loop execute?

2. How many times does the inner loop execute?

3. What is the value of sum printed by cout?

4. What would happen if you changed rows++ and columns++ to ++rows and ++columns?

LAB 5-5: NESTING LOOPS

In this lab, you add nested loops to a C++ program provided with the data files for this book. The program should print the outline of a rectangle, as shown in Figure 5-2. The rectangle is printed using asterisks, six across and eight down. Note that this program uses cout << "*"; to print an asterisk and cout << " " to print a space.

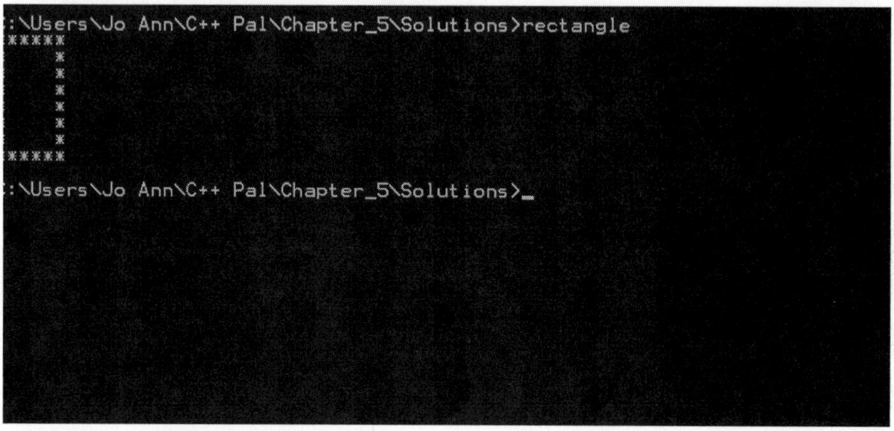

Figure 5-2 Rectangle printed by Rectangle.cpp

1. Open the source code file named Rectangle.cpp using Notepad or the text editor of your choice.

2. Write the nested loops to control the number of rows and the number of columns that make up the rectangle.

3. In the loop body, use a nested if statement to decide when to print an asterisk and when to print a space. The output statements have been written, but you must decide when and where to use them.

4. Save this source code file in a directory of your choice and then make that directory your working directory.

5. Compile the source code file Rectangle.cpp.

6. Execute the program. Your rectangle outline should look like the rectangle outline in Figure 5-2.

7. Modify the program to change the number of rows from six to eight and the number of columns from eight to 10. What does the rectangle look like now?

ACCUMULATING TOTALS IN A LOOP

You can use a loop in C++ to accumulate a total as your program executes. For example, assume that your computer science instructor has asked you to design and write a program that she can use to calculate an average score for the midterm exam she gave last week. To find the average test score, you need to add all the students' test scores, and then divide that sum by the number of students who took the midterm.

Note that the logic for this program should include a loop that will execute for each student in the class. In the loop, you get a student's test score as input and add that value to a total. After you get all of the test scores and accumulate the sum of all the test scores, you divide that sum by the number of students. You should plan to ask the user to input the number of student test scores that will be entered because your instructor wants to reuse this program using a different number of students each time it is executed.

As you review your work, you realize that the program will accumulate a sum within the loop and that you will also need to keep a count for the number of students. You learned in *Programming Logic and Design, Fifth Edition* that you add 1 to a counter each time a loop executes and that you add some other value to an accumulator. For this program, that other value added to the accumulator is a student's test score.

The following C++ program includes the loop required for this program. Notice that the loop body includes an accumulator and a counter.

```
// This program calculates an average test score given individual
// test scores.
// Input: Interactive - Student Test Scores
// Output: Number of Students taking the test and the test score
// average
#include <iostream>
#include <string>
using namespace std;
int main()
{
    // Declare variables
    int testScore;
    int numStudents;
    int stuCount;
    double testTotal;
    double average;
    // Get user input to control loop
    cout << "Enter number of students: ";
    cin >> numStudents;
    // Initialize accumulator variable to 0
    testTotal = 0;
    // Loop for each student
    for(stuCount = 0; stuCount < numStudents; stuCount++)
```

»NOTE
If testTotal is not initialized, it may contain an unknown value referred to as a "garbage" value. The C++ compiler issues a warning message for uninitialized variables.

```
{
    // Input student test score
    cout << "Enter student's score: ";
    cin >> testScore;
    // Accumulate total of test scores
    testTotal += testScore;
}
// Calculate average test score
average = testTotal / stuCount;
// Output number of students and average test score
cout << "Number of Students: " << stuCount << endl;
cout << "Average Test Score: " << average << endl;
return 0;
}
```

In the code, you use the cout statement to ask your user to tell you how many students took the test. Then you use cin to retrieve the user input and store it in the variable named numStudents. Next, the accumulator, testTotal, is initialized to 0.

After the accumulator is initialized, the code uses a for loop and the loop control variable, stuCount, to control the loop. A for loop is a good choice because, at this point in the program, you know how many times the loop should execute. You use the for loop's first expression to initialize stuCount, and then the second expression is evaluated to see if stuCount is less than numStudents. If this is true, the body of the loop executes, using cout and cin again, this time asking the user to enter a test score and retrieving the input and storing it in testScore.

> **»NOTE** You must calculate the average outside of the loop, not inside the loop. The only way you could calculate the average inside the loop is do it each time the loop executes, but this is inefficient.

Next, you must add the value of testScore to the accumulator, testTotal. The loop control variable, stuCount, is then incremented, and the incremented value is tested to see if it is less than numStudents. If this is true again, the loop executes a second time. The loop continues to execute until the value of stuCount < numStudents is false. Outside the for loop, you calculate the average test score by dividing testTotal by stuCount.

> **»NOTE** If a user enters a 0, meaning 0 students took the midterm, the for loop does not execute because the value of numStudents is 0 and the value of stuCount is also 0, and the first time the second expression in the for loop is evaluated, it is false.

The entire C++ program is saved in a file named TestAverage.cpp. You may want to study the source code, compile it, and execute the program to experience how accumulators and counters behave. The output from this program with five students whose test scores are 76, 65, 88, 90, and 92 is displayed in Figure 5-3.

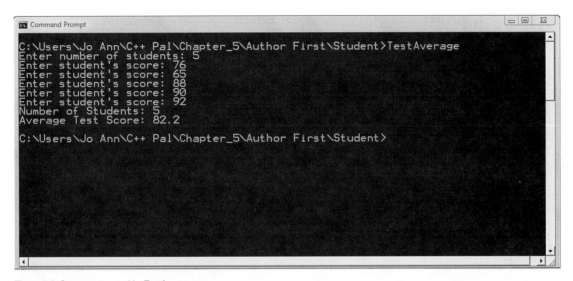

Figure 5-3 Output generated by TestAverage.cpp

EXERCISE 5-8: ACCUMULATING TOTALS IN A LOOP

In this exercise, you use what you have learned about using counters and accumulating totals in a loop. Study the C++ code that follows, and then answer the subsequent questions about the code. The complete program is saved in the file named `Rainfall.cpp`. You may want to compile and execute the program to help you answer these questions.

```cpp
const int DAYS_IN_WEEK = 7;
for(counter = 1; counter <= DAYS_IN_WEEK; counter++)
{
    cout << "Enter rainfall amount for Day " + counter << endl;
    cin >> rainfall;
    cout << "Day " << counter << "rainfall amount is " <<
            rainfall << " inches" << endl;
    sum += rainfall;
}
// calculate average
average = sum / DAYS_IN_WEEK;
```

1. What happens when you compile this program if the variable sum is not initialized with the value 0?

   _____

2. Could you replace sum += rainfall; with sum = sum + rainfall; ?

   _____

3. The variables sum, rainfall, and average should be declared to be what data type to calculate the most accurate average rainfall?

_____

4. Could you replace DAYS_IN_WEEK in the statement average = sum / DAYS_IN_WEEK; with the variable named counter and still get the desired result? Explain.

_____

_____

LAB 5-6: ACCUMULATING TOTALS IN A LOOP

In this lab, you add a statement to a loop body in a C++ program provided with the data files for this book. When completed, the statement you add should calculate the total daily sales for a book store. The loop executes until the user enters the word "done" instead of a book title. After the user enters a book title, he or she is asked to enter the transaction amount. The transaction amounts are listed in Table 5-1.

Book Title	Transaction Amount
Harry Potter and the Deathly Hallows	$17.99
A Thousand Splendid Suns	$14.99
The Dangerous Book for Boys	$14.99
Eat, Pray, Love	$ 9.00
Marley and Me	$14.99
The Tipping Point	$ 8.99
Fahrenheit 451	$ 4.99

Table 5-1 Input for Lab 5-6

Note that variables have been declared for you and the input statements and all but one output statement have been written. In this lab, you will add the output statement that displays the bookstore's total daily sales and you will calculate a total of daily sales for the bookstore.

1. Open the source code file named BookSales.cpp using Notepad or the text editor of your choice.

2. Add a statement to the loop body that allows you to calculate a total of daily sales for the bookstore.

3. Save this source code file in a directory of your choice and then make that directory your working directory.

4. Compile the source code file `BookSales.cpp`.

5. Execute the program using the data listed in Table 5-1. Record the sum of daily book sales.

_____

_____

USING A LOOP TO VALIDATE INPUT

In Chapter 5 of *Programming Logic and Design, Fifth Edition*, you learned that you cannot count on users to enter valid data in programs that ask them to enter data. You also learned that you should validate input from your user so you can avoid problems caused by invalid input.

If your program requires a user to enter a specific value, such as a "Y" or an "N" in response to a question, then your program should validate that your user entered an exact match to either "Y" or "N". If not, you must decide what action to take in your program. As an example of testing for an exact match, consider the following code:

```
string answer;
cout << "Do you want to continue? Enter Y or N.   ";
cin >> answer;
while(answer != "Y" && answer != "N")
{
    cout << "Invalid Response. Please type Y or N.   ";
    cin >> answer;
}
```

In the example, the variable named `answer` contains your user's answer to the question "`Do you want to continue? Enter Y or N.`". In the expression that is part of the `while` loop, you test to see if your user really did enter a "Y" or an "N". If not, you enter the loop, tell the user he or she entered invalid input, and then request that he or she type a "Y" or an "N". The expression in the `while` loop is tested again to see if the user entered valid data this time. If not, the loop body executes again and continues to execute until the user enters valid input.

You can also verify user input in a program that requests a user to enter numeric data. For example, your program could ask a user to enter a number in the range of 1 to 4. It is very important to verify this numeric input, especially if your program uses the input in arithmetic calculations. What would happen if the user entered a 0 instead of the number 1? Or, what would happen if the user entered 100? More than likely, your program will not run correctly. The following code example illustrates how you can verify that a user enters correct numeric data:

```
int answer;
const int MIN_NUM = 1;
const int MAX_NUM = 4;
cout << "Please enter a number in the range of " << MIN_NUM <<
        " to " << MAX_NUM << ": ";
cin >> answer;
while(answer < MIN_NUM || answer > MAX_NUM)
{
    cout << "Number must be between " << MIN_NUM << " and " <<
            MAX_NUM << ". Please try again: ";
    cin >> answer;
}
```

EXERCISE 5-9: VALIDATING USER INPUT

In this exercise, you use what you have learned about validating user input to answer the following questions:

1. You plan to use the following statement in a C++ program to validate user input:

```
while(inputString == "")
```

What would your user enter to cause this test to be `true`?

_____

2. You plan to use the following statement in a C++ program to validate user input:

```
while(userAnswer == "Y" || userAnswer == "y")
```

What would a user enter to cause this test to be `true`?

_____

3. You plan to use the following statement in a C++ program to validate user input:

```
while(userAnswer < 6 || userAnswer > 12)
```

What would a user enter to cause this test to be `true`?

_____

LAB 5-7: VALIDATING USER INPUT

In this lab, you make additions to a C++ program provided with the data files for this book. The program is a guessing game. A random number between 1 and 10 is generated in the program. The user enters a number between 1 and 10, trying to guess the correct number. If the user guesses correctly, the program congratulates the user, and then the loop that controls guessing numbers exits; otherwise the program asks the user if he or she wants to guess again. If the user enters a "Y", you let him or her guess again. If the user enters "N", the loop exits. You can see that the user entering a "Y" or an "N" is the sentinel value that controls the loop. Note that the entire program has been written for you. You need to add code that validates correct input, which is a Y or an N when the user is asked if he or she wants to guess a number, and a number in the range of 1 through 10 when the user is asked to guess a number.

1. Open the source code file named GuessNumber.cpp using Notepad or the text editor of your choice.

2. Write loops that validate input at all places in the code where the user is asked to provide input. Comments have been included in the code to help you identify where these loops should be written.

3. Save this source code file in a directory of your choice and then make that directory your working directory.

4. Compile the source code file GuessNumber.cpp.

5. Execute the program. See if you can guess the randomly generated number. Execute the program several times to see if the random number changes. Also, test the program to verify that incorrect input is handled correctly. On your best attempt, how many guesses did you have to take to guess the correct number? _____

6

USING ARRAYS IN C++ PROGRAMS

After studying this chapter, you will be able to:

Use arrays in C++ programs
Search an array for a value
Use parallel arrays in a C++ program

You should do the exercises and labs in this chapter after you have finished Chapter 6 of *Programming Logic and Design, Fifth Edition*, by Joyce Farrell. In this chapter, you learn how to use C++ to declare and initialize arrays. You then access the elements of an array to assign values and process them within your program. You also learn why it is important to stay within the bounds of an array. In addition, you study some programs written in C++ that implement the logic and design presented in *Programming Logic and Design, Fifth Edition*.

ARRAY BASICS

An **array** is a group of data items in which all items have the same data type, are referenced using the same variable name, and are stored in consecutive memory locations. To reference an individual element in an array, you use a subscript. Think of a **subscript** as the position number of a value within an array. It is important for you to know that in C++, subscript values begin with 0 (zero) and end with n-1, where n is the number of items stored in the array.

To use an array in a C++ program, you must first learn how to declare an array, initialize an array with predetermined values, access array elements, and stay within the bounds of an array. In the next section you'll focus on the first step, declaring arrays.

DECLARING ARRAYS

Before you can use an array in a C++ program, you must first declare it. That is, you must give it a name and specify the data type for the data that will be stored in it. In some cases, you also specify the number of items that will be stored in the array. The following code shows how to declare an array named cityPopulations that will be used to store four ints, and an array named cities that will be used to store four strings:

```
int cityPopulations[4];
string cities[4];
```

As you can see in this example, you begin by specifying the data type of the items that will be stored in the array. The data type is followed by the name of the array and then a pair of square brackets. Within the square brackets, you see an integer value that specifies the number of elements this array can hold.

As shown in Figure 6-1, the compiler allocates enough consecutive memory locations to store four elements of data type int for the array named cityPopulations. If cityPopulations[0] is stored at memory address 1000, then the address of cityPopulations[1] is 1004 because each int requires 4 bytes of memory. Similarly, cityPopulations[3] is at address 1012.

```
int cityPopulations[4];
```

```
[0]                        [3]
Memory                     Memory
Address                    Address
1000                       1012
```

> **▶▶ NOTE**
> If an array is declared to store items of data type double, 8 bytes are allocated for each item in the array.

Figure 6-1 Memory allocation for cityPopulations array

The `cityPopulations` array provides an example of how memory is allocated for arrays that contain primitive data types. Memory allocation is different for arrays of `strings` because a `string` is an object in C++, not a primitive data type. Using the Visual C++ compiler and Windows Vista, 28 bytes of memory are allocated for a `string` object. This represents the size of the object.

Additional memory for the characters that make up the string might be allocated **dynamically** (as your program runs) when a value is stored in the `string` object. This is shown in Figure 6-2.

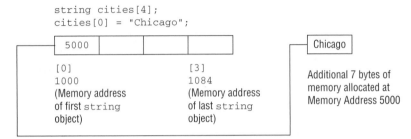

Figure 6-2 Memory allocation for `cities` array

In Figure 6-2, the compiler allocates enough consecutive memory locations to store four `string` objects for the array named `cities`. If the address of `cities[0]` is 1000, the address of `cities[1]` is 1028, and the address of `cities[3]` is 1084 because each reference requires 28 bytes of memory. When a string is assigned to `cities[0]`, memory is dynamically allocated at another memory address. This address is then stored in the array. When the statement `cities[0] = "Chicago";` executes, the memory dynamically allocated for Chicago begins at address 5000 and then that address (5000) is stored in the first element of the array. An example of creating `string` objects is presented later in this chapter.

INITIALIZING ARRAYS

In C++, array elements are not automatically initialized to any value when the array is declared. Therefore, all of the elements of an array contain a **garbage value**, which means they contain the values last stored at the memory location assigned to your array. Because these values are not useful in your program, it is a good idea to initialize arrays to all zeros for arrays that store numbers and to empty strings for arrays that store strings. Two double quotes with no space between, `""`, is the empty string in C++.

You can and will sometimes want to initialize arrays with values that you choose. You do this when you declare the array. To initialize an array when you declare it, use curly braces to surround a comma-delimited list of data items, as shown in the following example:

```
int cityPopulations[] = {9500000, 871100, 23900, 40100};
string cities[] = {"Chicago", "Detroit", "Batavia", "Lima"};
```

You can also use assignment statements to provide values for array elements after an array is declared, as in the following example:

```
cityPopulations[0] = 9500000;
cities[0] = "Chicago";
```

A loop is often used to assign values to the elements in an array, as shown here:

```cpp
int loopIndex;
for(loopIndex = 0; loopIndex < 3; loopIndex++)
{
    cityPopulations[loopIndex] = 12345;
    cities[loopIndex] = "AnyCity";
}
```

The first time this loop is encountered, loopIndex is assigned the value 0. Because 0 is less than 3, the body of the loop executes, assigning the value 12345 to cityPopulations[0] and the value "AnyCity" to cities[0]. Next, the value of loopIndex is incremented and takes on the value 1. Because 1 is less than 3, the loop executes a second time and the value 12345 is assigned to cityPopulations[1] and "AnyCity" is assigned to cities[1]. Each time the loop executes, the value of loopIndex is incremented. This allows you to access a different location in the arrays each time the body of the loop executes.

▶▶ NOTE
Remember that subscript values begin with 0 (zero) in C++.

ACCESSING ARRAY ELEMENTS

You need to access individual locations in an array when you assign a value to an array element, print its value, change its value, assign the value to another variable, and so forth. In C++, you use an integer expression placed in square brackets to indicate which element in the array you want to access. This integer expression is the subscript.

▶▶ NOTE
Later in this chapter, you will learn to use a named constant in an array declaration.

The following C++ program declares two arrays of data type double, initializes an array of data type double, copies values from one array to another, changes several values stored in the array named target, and prints the values of the arrays named source and target. You can compile and execute this program if you like. It is stored in the file named ArrayTest.cpp. Figure 6-3 shows the output generated by the ArrayTest program.

```cpp
#include <iostream>
#include <string>
using namespace std;
int main()
{
    double target[3];
    double source[] = {1.0, 5.5, 7.9};
    int loopIndex;
    // Copy values from source to target
    for(loopIndex = 0; loopIndex < 3; loopIndex++)
        target[loopIndex] = source[loopIndex];
    // Assign values to two elements of target
    target[0] = 2.0;
    target[1] = 4.5;
    // Print values stored in source and target
    for(loopIndex = 0; loopIndex < 3; loopIndex++)
    {
        cout << "Source " << source[loopIndex] << endl;
        cout << "Target " << target[loopIndex] << endl;
    }
}
```

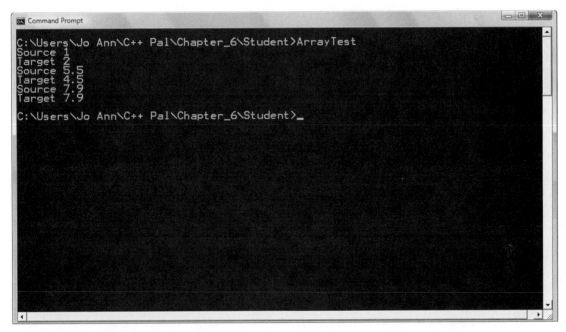

Figure 6-3 Output generated by the ArrayTest program

STAYING WITHIN THE BOUNDS OF AN ARRAY

As a C++ programmer, you must be careful to ensure that the subscript values you use to access array elements are within the legal bounds. Unlike most other programming languages, the C++ compiler does *not* check to make sure that a subscript used in your program is greater than or equal to 0 and less than the length of the array. For example, suppose you declare an array named numbers as follows:

```
int numbers[10];
```

In this case, the C++ compiler does not check to make sure the subscripts you use to access this array are integer values between 0 and 9.

>> **NOTE** When using a loop to access the elements in an array, be sure that the test you use to terminate the loop keeps you within the legal bounds, 0 to *n*-1, where *n* is the number of items stored in the array.

However, when you execute your program, if you use an array subscript that is not in the legal bounds, a garbage value is accessed. As an example, consider the highlighted operator in the following code, which is taken from the previous C++ program example:

```
double source[] = {1.0, 5.5, 7.9};
int loopIndex;
for(loopIndex = 0; loopIndex < 3; loopIndex++)
```

If you change the highlighted operator to <=, as shown here, your program will compile with no errors:

```
for(loopIndex = 0; loopIndex <= 3; loopIndex++)
```

A problem arises, however, when your program runs because the loop will execute when the value of `loopIndex` is 3. When you access the array element `source[3]`, you are outside the bounds of the array because there is no such element in this array and a garbage value is stored at this location in the array.

USING CONSTANTS WITH ARRAYS

» NOTE
It is a C++ convention to use all capital letters when naming constants.

It is a good programming practice to use a named constant to help you stay within the bounds of an array when you write programs that declare and access arrays. The following example shows how to use a named constant:

```
const int NUM_ITEMS = 3;
double target[NUM_ITEMS];
int loopIndex;
for(loopIndex = 0; loopIndex < NUM_ITEMS; loopIndex++)
        target[loopIndex] = loopIndex + 10;
```

EXERCISE 6-1: ARRAY BASICS

Use what you have learned about declaring and initializing arrays to complete the following:

1. Write array declarations for each of the following:

    a. Seven paycheck values

    _____

    b. Two movie titles

    _____

    c. Eleven whole numbers

    _____

2. Declare and initialize arrays that store the following:

    a. The ages 25, 33, 5, 60, and 32

    _____

    b. The names Jeanne, Karen, and William

    _____

    c. The prices 5.00, 35.00, and 4.50

    _____

3. Write an assignment statement that assigns the value 35 to the first element of the array of integers named `miles`.

4. An array of `ints` named `numbers` is stored at memory location 4000. Where is `numbers[1]`? Where is `numbers[10]`?

LAB 6-1: USING ARRAYS

In this lab, you complete a partially prewritten C++ program that uses an array. The program prompts the user to enter 10 integer values and store them in an array. It should then find the minimum and maximum values stored in the array as well as the average of the 10 values. The data file provided for this lab includes the input statement and some variables declarations. Comments are included in the file to help you write the remainder of the program.

1. Open the source code file named `MinMax.cpp` using Notepad or the text editor of your choice.

2. Write the C++ statements as indicated by the comments.

3. Save this source code file in a directory of your choice and then make that directory your working directory.

4. Compile the source code file `MinMax.cpp`.

5. Execute the program.

> **NOTE**
> Notice that the equality operator `==` is used when comparing the `int` value in the first `if` statement and the `bool` value in the second `if` statement.

SEARCHING AN ARRAY
FOR AN EXACT MATCH

One of the programs described in *Programming Logic and Design, Fifth Edition* uses an array to hold valid item numbers for a mail-order business. The idea is that when a customer orders an item, you can determine if the customer ordered a valid item number by searching through the array for that item number. This program relies on a technique called setting a flag to verify that an item exists in an array. The pseudocode and the C++ code for this program are shown in Figure 6-4.

> **NOTE**
> The program can be found in the file named `MailOrder.cpp`. You may want to compile and execute the program to see how it operates.

```
start
    string name
    string address
    num item
    num quantity
    num SIZE = 6
    num VALID_ITEM[SIZE] = 106, 108, 307, 405, 457, 688
    num sub
    string foundIt = "N"
    string MSG_YES = "Item available"
    string MSG_NO = "Item not found"
    get name, address, item, quantity
    sub = 0
    while sub < SIZE
        if item = VALID_ITEM[sub] then
            foundIt = "Y"
        endif
        sub = sub + 1
    endwhile
    if foundIt = "Y"
        print MSG_YES
    else
        print MSG_NO
    endif
stop
```

```cpp
#include <iostream>
#include <string>
using namespace std;

int main()
{
   // Declare variables
   const int STR_LENGTH = 80;
   char name[STR_LENGTH], address[STR_LENGTH];
   int item, quantity;
   const int SIZE = 6;
   int valid_item[] = {106, 108, 307, 405, 457, 688};
   int sub;
   bool foundIt = false;
   const string MSG_YES = "Item Available";
   const string MSG_NO = "Item not found";
```

Figure 6-4 Pseudocode and C++ code for mail-order program ▶

```
// Get user input
cout << "Enter name: ";
cin.getline(name, STR_LENGTH);
cout << "Enter address: ";
cin.getline(address, STR_LENGTH);
cout << "Enter item number: ";
cin >> item;
cout << "Enter quantity: ";
cin >> quantity;
// Initialize loop index to 0
sub = 0;
// Loop through array
while(sub < SIZE)
{
   // Test to see if this item is a valid item
   if(item == valid_item[sub])
      foundIt = true;    // Set flag to true
   sub += 1;             // Increment loop index
}
// Test value of foundIt
if(foundIt == true)
   cout << MSG_YES << endl;
else
   cout << MSG_NO << endl;
return 0;
}
```

Figure 6-4 Pseudocode and C++ code for mail-order program (*continued*)

As shown in Figure 6-4, when you translate the pseudocode to C++, you make a few changes. In both the pseudocode and the C++ code, the variable named foundIt is the flag. However, in the C++ code you assign the value false instead of the string constant "N" to the variable named foundIt. This is because the variable named foundIt is declared as a variable of the bool type. The bool data type is one of C++'s primitive data types and is only used to store true and false values.

Also, notice the pseudocode includes one statement to get the user's name, address, item, and quantity, whereas it takes many statements in C++ to get the user's input.

NOTE
The variable named foundIt could be declared as a string as it was in the pseudocode. It is better to use a bool in C++ for true and false values.

NOTE Notice the mail-order program uses character arrays, not strings, to store the customer's name and address. Character arrays must be used because the program uses the getline() function to retrieve the user's input for name and address. You will learn about using character arrays to store strings and using the getline() function as you learn more about C++.

EXERCISE 6-2: SEARCHING AN ARRAY FOR AN EXACT MATCH

Using what you have learned about searching an array for an exact match, study the following C++ code and then answer the questions. Note that this code may contain errors.

```
string states[] = {"Illinois", "Ohio", "Iowa", "Texas"};
int foundIt = false, i;
const int MAX_STATES = 4;
string inState;
cout << "Enter state name:";
cin >> instate;
for(i = 0; i <= MAX_STATES; i++)
{
    if(inState == states[i])
    {
        foundIt = true;
    }
}
```

1. Is the `for` loop written correctly?

   _____

   If not, how can you fix it?

   _____

2. Which variable is the flag?

   _____

3. Is the flag variable declared correctly?

   _____

   If not, what should you do to fix it?

   _____

4. Is the comparison in the `if` statement done correctly?

   _____

   If not, how can you fix it?

   _____

LAB 6-2: SEARCHING AN ARRAY FOR AN EXACT MATCH

In this lab, you use what you have learned about searching an array to find an exact match to complete a partially prewritten C++ program. The program uses an array that contains valid area codes for 10 cities in the United States. You ask the user of the program to enter an area code; your program then searches the array for that area code. If it is not found, the program should print a message that informs the user that the area code is not found in the list of valid area codes.

The data file provided for this lab includes the input statements and the necessary variable declarations. You need to use a loop to examine all the items in the array and test for a match. You also need to set a flag if there is a match and then test the flag variable to determine if you should print the "Area code not found." message. Comments in the code tell you where to write your statements. You can use the mail-order program in this chapter as a guide.

1. Open the source code file named `AreaCodes.cpp` using Notepad or the text editor of your choice.

2. Study the prewritten code to make sure you understand it.

3. Write a loop statement that examines the area codes stored in the array.

4. Write code that tests for a match.

5. Write code that, when appropriate, prints the message "Area code not found."

6. Save this source code file in a directory of your choice and then make that directory your working directory.

7. Compile the source code file `AreaCodes.cpp`.

8. Execute the program using the following as input:

    269

    512

    312

    708

PARALLEL ARRAYS

As you learned in *Programming Logic and Design, Fifth Edition*, you use parallel arrays to store values and to maintain a relationship between the items stored in the arrays. Figure 6-5 shows that the student ID number stored in `stuID[0]` and the grade stored in `grades[0]` are related—student 56 received a grade of 99.

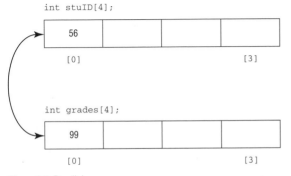

Figure 6-5 Parallel arrays

NOTE
Parallel arrays have the same number of elements but they do not necessarily store items of the same data type.

This relationship is established by using the same subscript value when accessing each array. Note that as the programmer, you must maintain this relationship in your code by always using the same subscript. C++ does not create or maintain the relationship.

One of the programs discussed in *Programming Logic and Design, Fifth Edition* is an expanded version of the mail-order program discussed in the "Searching an Array for an Exact Match" section earlier in this chapter. In this expanded program, you want to determine the price of the ordered item, multiply that price by the quantity ordered, and print a bill. You use parallel arrays to help you organize the data for the program. One array, valid_item, contains six valid item numbers. The other array, valid_item_price, contains six valid prices. Each price is in the same position as the corresponding item number in the other array. When a customer orders an item, you search the valid_item array for the customer's item number. When the item number is found, you use the price stored in the same location of the valid_item_price array to calculate the customer's bill. The complete C++ program is stored in the file named MailOrder2.cpp. The pseudocode and C++ code that search the valid_item array and use a price from the valid_item_price array to calculate the customer's bill are shown in Figure 6-6.

```
start
   string name
   string address
   num item
   num quantity
   num price
   num SIZE = 6
   num VALID_ITEM[SIZE] = 106, 108, 307, 405, 457, 688
   num VALID_ITEM_PRICE[SIZE] = 0.59, 0.99, 4.50, 15.99, 17.50, 39.00
   num sub
   string foundIt = "N"
   string MSG_YES = "Item available"
   string MSG_NO = "Item not found"
   get name, address, item, quantity
   sub = 0
   while sub < SIZE
     if item = VALID_ITEM[sub] then
        foundIt = "Y"
        price = VALID_ITEM_PRICE[sub]
     endif
     sub = sub + 1
   endwhile
   if foundIt = "Y"
     print MSG_YES
     print quantity, " at ", price, " each"
     print "Total ", quantity * price
   else
     print MSG_NO
   endif
stop
```

Figure 6-6 Pseudocode and C++ code for expanded mail-order program ▶

```cpp
#include <iostream>
#include <string>
using namespace std;

int main()
{
    // Declare variables
    const int STR_LENGTH = 80;
    char name[STR_LENGTH], address[STR_LENGTH];
    int item, quantity;
    double price = 0.0;
    const int SIZE = 6;
    int valid_item[] = {106, 108, 307, 405, 457, 688};
    double valid_item_price[] = {0.59, 0.99, 4.50, 15.99, 17.50, 39.00};
    int sub;
    bool foundIt = false;
    const string MSG_YES = "Item Available";
    const string MSG_NO = "Item not found";

    // Get user input
    cout << "Enter name: ";
    cin.getline(name, STR_LENGTH);
    cout << "Enter address: ";
    cin.getline(address, STR_LENGTH);
    cout << "Enter item number: ";
    cin >> item;
    cout << "Enter quantity: ";
    cin >> quantity;
    // Initialize loop index to 0
    sub = 0;
    // Loop through array
    while(sub < SIZE)
    {
        // Test to see if this item is a valid item
        if(item == valid_item[sub])
        {
            foundIt = true; // Set flag to true
            price = valid_item_price[sub]; // Get price from parallel array
        }
        sub += 1;                       // Increment loop index
}
```

Figure 6-6 Pseudocode and C++ code for expanded mail-order program (*continued*) ▶

```
    // Test value of foundIt
    if(foundIt == true)
    {
        cout << MSG_YES << endl;
        cout << quantity << " at " << price << " each" << endl;
        cout << "Total " << quantity * price << endl;
    }
    else
        cout << MSG_NO << endl;

    return 0;
}
```

Figure 6-6 Pseudocode and C++ code for expanded mail-order program (*continued*)

EXERCISE 6-3: PARALLEL ARRAYS

Use what you have learned about parallel arrays to evaluate the following code and then answer the questions:

```
string cities[] = "Batavia", "Gary", "Westmont", "Plano";
int populations[] = 23900, 102700, 24300, 5700;
const int MAX_CITIES = 4;
int saveIt;
int i, x;
string inCity;
cout << "Enter city name: ";
cin >> inCity;

for(i = 0; i = MAX_CITIES; ++i)
{
    if(inCity == cities[i])
    {
        saveIt = i;
    }
}
cout << "Population for " << cities[saveIt] <<
        " is " << populations[saveIt] << endl;
```

1. Are the arrays declared and initialized correctly?

   _____

   If not, how can you fix them?

   _____

2. Is the `for` loop written correctly?

_____

If not, how can you fix it?

_____

3. As written, how many times will the `for` loop execute?

_____

4. How would you describe the purpose of the statement `saveIt = i;`?

_____

LAB 6-3: PARALLEL ARRAYS

In this lab, you use what you have learned about parallel arrays to complete a partially completed C++ program. The program is described in Chapter 6, Exercise 6 in *Programming Logic and Design, Fifth Edition*. The program should either print the name and price for a fast-food item from the Billy Goat Fast Food Restaurant or it should print the message "Sorry, we do not carry that."

Read the problem description carefully before you begin. The data file provided for this lab includes the necessary variable declarations and input statements. You need to write the part of the program that searches for the name of the food item and either prints its name and price or prints the error message if the item is not found. Comments in the code tell you where to write your statements. You can use the expanded mail-order program shown in Figure 6-6 as a guide.

1. Open the source code file named `BillyGoat.cpp` using Notepad or the text editor of your choice.

2. Study the prewritten code to make sure you understand it.

3. Write the code that searches the array for the name of the food item ordered by the customer.

4. Write the code that prints the name and price of the food item or the error message.

5. Save this source code file in a directory of your choice and then make that directory your working directory.

6. Compile the source code file `BillyGoat.cpp`.

》NOTE
Remember that
C++ is case sensi-
tive, which means
it distinguishes
between upper-
case letters and
lowercase letters.

7. Execute the program using the following data and record the output:

Customer Number	Item Ordered
123	Fries
234	Pepsi
345	Coffee
456	Chips
567	Rings
678	Coke
789	Hamburger

CHAPTER

7

USING FUNCTIONS
IN C++ PROGRAMS

After studying this chapter, you will be able to:

Write functions that require a single parameter
Write functions that require multiple parameters
Write functions that return values
Pass entire arrays and single elements of an array
   to a function
Pass arguments to functions by reference and by
   address
Overload functions
Use C++ built-in functions

In Chapter 3 of this book, you learned that local variables are variables that are declared within the function that uses them. You also learned that most programs consist of a main function that contains the mainline logic and then calls other functions to get specific work done in the program.

In this chapter, you learn more about functions in C++. You learn how to write functions that require a single parameter, how to write functions that require multiple parameters, and how to write functions that return a value. You also learn how to pass an array to a function, how to pass arguments by reference and by address, how to overload a function, and how to use some of C++'s built-in functions. To help you learn about functions, you will study some C++ programs that implement the logic and design presented in *Programming Logic and Design, Fifth Edition* by Joyce Farrell.

You should do the exercises and labs in this chapter after you have finished Chapter 7 of *Programming Logic and Design, Fifth Edition*.

A SIMPLE C++ FUNCTION

To review what you already learned about functions, we review the C++ code for the Customer Bill program from Chapter 3 in this book. This program is shown in Figure 7-1. Notice the line numbers in front of each line of code in this program. These line numbers are not actually part of the program but are included for reference only.

```
1    /* Program Name: CustomerBill.cpp
2       Function: This program uses a function to print a company name and address
3       and then prints a customer name and balance.
4       Input:   Interactive
5       Output: Company name and address, customer name and balance
6    */
7    #include <iostream>
8    #include <string>
9    void nameAndAddress(); // function declaration
10   using namespace std;
11   int main()
12   {
13      // Declare variables local to main
14      string firstName;
15      string lastName;
16      double balance;
17
18      // Get interactive input
19      cout << "Enter customer's first name: ";
20      cin >> firstName;
21      cout << "Enter customer's last name: ";
22      cin >> lastName;
23      cout << "Enter customer's balance: ";
24      cin >> balance;
```

Figure 7-1 C++ code for Customer Bill program ▶

```
25
26          // Call nameAndAddress function
27          nameAndAddress();
28          // Output customer name and address
29          cout << "Customer Name:   " << firstName << " " << lastName << endl;
30          cout << "Customer Balance:   " << balance << endl;
31
32          return 0;
33     } // End of main function
34
35     void nameAndAddress()
36     {
37          // Declare and initialize local, constant Strings
38          const string ADDRESS_LINE1 = "ABC Manufacturing";
39          const string ADDRESS_LINE2 = "47 Industrial Lane";
40          const string ADDRESS_LINE3 = "Wild Rose, WI 54984";
41
42          // Output
43          cout << ADDRESS_LINE1 << endl;
44          cout << ADDRESS_LINE2 << endl;
45          cout << ADDRESS_LINE3 << endl;
46     }  // End of nameAndAddress function
```

Figure 7-1 C++ code for Customer Bill program (*continued*)

On lines 1-6, you see a multiline comment that describes the Customer Bill program followed by two #include preprocessor directives on lines 7 and 8 that give the program the ability to perform input and output and the ability to use strings. On line 9, you see the function declaration for the nameAndAddress function. As with variables in C++, you must declare a function before you can call the function in your program. A **function declaration** (also known as a **function prototype**) should specify the data type of the value the function returns, the name of the function, and the data type of each of its arguments. On line 9 you see that the nameAndAddress function returns nothing (void) and expects no arguments.

The program begins execution with the main function, which is shown on line 11. This function contains the declaration of three variables (lines 14, 15, and 16), firstName, lastName, and balance, which are local to the main function. Next, on lines 19 through 24, interactive input statements retrieve values for firstName, lastName, and balance. The function nameAndAddress is then called on line 27, with no arguments listed within its parentheses. Remember that **arguments**, which are sometimes called **actual parameters**, are data items sent to functions. There are no arguments for the nameAndAddress function because this function requires no data. You will learn about passing arguments to functions later in this chapter. The last two statements (lines 29 and 30) in the main function are print statements that output the customer's firstName, lastName, and balance.

Next, on line 35, you see the header for the nameAndAddress function. The **header** begins with the void keyword, followed by the function name, which is nameAndAddress. As you learned in Chapter 1 of this book, the void keyword indicates that the nameAndAddress function does not return a value. You learn more about functions that return values later in this chapter.

Also, notice that there are no formal parameters within the parentheses. Remember that **formal parameters** are the variables in the function header that accept the values from the actual parameters. (You will learn about writing functions that accept parameters in the next section of this chapter.) In the next part of the Customer Bill program, we see three constants that are local to the nameAndAddress function: ADDRESS_LINE1, ADDRESS_LINE2, and ADDRESS_LINE3. These constants are declared and initialized on lines 38, 39, and 40, and then printed on lines 43, 44, and 45.

Now that you have reviewed the basics of writing a simple function in C++, you are ready to learn something new. In the next section you will learn how to write functions that require a single parameter.

EXERCISE 7-1: WRITING SIMPLE FUNCTIONS

In this exercise, you use what you have learned about writing simple functions in C++.

1. Given the following function calls, write the function's header and function declaration:

   a. printBirthdayInvitation();

   _____

   b. displayHeader();

   _____

   c. displayInstructions();

   _____

2. Given the following function headers, write a function call:

   a. void displayStoreName()

   _____

   b. void printTemplate()

   _____

   c. void displayPhoneBook()

   _____

LAB 7-1: WRITING SIMPLE FUNCTIONS

In this lab, you complete a partially prewritten C++ program that includes simple functions. The program prompts the user for his or her age. If the user is 21 or older, the program should call a function named allowEntry that displays the message "You are old enough to enter this establishment." If the user is younger than 21, the program should call a function named doNotAllowEntry that displays the message "Sorry, you'll have to wait until you are 21." The source code file provided for this lab includes the necessary variable declarations and the input statement. Comments are included in the file to help you write the remainder of the program.

1. Open the source code file named AllowEntry.cpp using Notepad or the text editor of your choice.

2. Write the C++ statements as indicated by the comments.

3. Save this source code file in a directory of your choice and then make that directory your working directory.

4. Compile the source code file, AllowEntry.cpp.

5. Execute the program.

WRITING FUNCTIONS THAT REQUIRE A SINGLE PARAMETER

As you learned in *Programming Logic and Design, Fifth Edition*, some functions require data to accomplish their task. You also learned that designing a program so that it sends data (which can be different each time the program runs) to a function (which doesn't change) keeps you from having to write multiple functions to handle similar situations. For example, suppose you are writing a program that has to determine if a number is even or odd. It is certainly better to write a single function, to which the program can pass a number entered by the user, than to write individual functions for every number.

In Figure 7-2, you see the C++ code for a program that includes a function that can determine if a number is odd or even. The line numbers are not actually part of the program but are included for reference only. The program allows the user to enter a number, and then passes that number to a function as an argument. After it receives the argument, the function can determine if the number is an even number or an odd number.

```
1     // EvenOrOdd.cpp - This program determines if a number input by the user is an
2     // even number or an odd number.
3     // Input:   Interactive
4     // Output:  The number entered and whether it is even or odd
5
6     #include <iostream>
7     #include <string>
8     void evenOrOdd(int);
9     using namespace std;
10
11    int main()
12    {
13       int number;
14       cout << "Enter a number or 999 to quit: ";
15       cin >> number;
16
17       while(number != 999)
18       {
19          evenOrOdd(number);
20          cout << "Enter a number or 999 to quit: ";
21          cin >> number;
22       }
23       return 0;
24    } // End of main function
25
26    void evenOrOdd(int number)
27    {
28       if((number % 2) == 0)
29          cout << "Number: " << number << " is even." << endl;
30       else
31          cout << "Number: " << number << " is odd." << endl;
32    } // End of evenOrOdd function
```

> The variable named `number` is local to the main function. Its value is stored at one memory location. For example, it may be stored at memory location 2000.

> The value of the formal parameter, `number`, is stored at a different memory location and is local to the `evenOrOdd` function. For example, it may be stored at memory location 7800.

Figure 7-2 C++ code for even or odd number program

On line 14 in this program, the user is asked to enter a number or the sentinel value, 999, when she is finished entering numbers and wants to quit the program. (You learned about sentinel values in Chapter 5 of this book.) On line 15, the input value is retrieved and then stored in the variable named `number`. Next, if the user did not enter the sentinel value 999, the `while` loop is entered and the function named `evenOrOdd` is called (line 19) using the following syntax:

```
evenOrOdd(number);
```

Notice that the `int` variable `number` is placed within the parentheses, which means that the value of `number` is passed to the `evenOrOdd` function. This is referred to as passing an argument by value. **Passing an argument by value** means that a copy of the value of the argument is passed to the function. Within the function, the value is stored

>> **NOTE**
Notice the function declaration on line 8 specifies that the `evenOrOdd` function does not return a value (`void`) and expects a single argument of data type `int`.

in the formal parameter at a different memory location, and is considered local to that function. In this example, as shown on line 26, the value is stored in the formal parameter named `number`.

The header for the `evenOrOdd` function on line 26 includes the `void` keyword, so you know the function will not return a value. The name of the function follows and within the parentheses that follow the function name, the parameter `number` is given a local name and declared as the `int` data type.

Remember that even though the parameter `number` has the same name as the local variable `number` in the `main` function, the values are stored at different memory locations. Figure 7-2 illustrates that the variable `number` that is local to `main` is stored at one memory location and the parameter `number` in the `evenOrOdd` function is stored at a different memory location.

Within the function on line 28, the modulus operator `%` is used in the test portion of the `if` statement to determine if the value of the local `number` is even or odd. The user is then informed if `number` is even (line 29) or odd (line 31), and program control is transferred back to the statement that follows the call to `evenOrOdd` in the `main` function (line 20).

Back in the `main` function, the user is asked to enter another number on line 20 and the `while` loop continues to execute, calling the `evenOrOdd` function with a new input value. The loop is exited when the user enters the sentinel value `999` and the program ends.

In the next section, you will learn how to pass more than one value to a function.

EXERCISE 7-2: WRITING FUNCTIONS THAT REQUIRE A SINGLE PARAMETER

In this exercise, you use what you have learned about writing functions that require a single parameter in C++.

1. Given the following variable declarations and function calls, write the function's header and function declaration:

   a. `string name;`

   `printBirthdayInvitation(name);`

   _____

   b. `double side_length;`

   `displaySquareArea(side_length);`

   _____

   c. `int month;`

   `displayDaysInMonth(month);`

   _____

2. Given the following function headers and variable declarations, write a function call:

a. `string store = "Walgreens";`

   `void displayStoreName(string storeName)`

   _____

b. `int currentYear;`

   `void printCalendar(int year)`

   _____

c. `string empID;`

   `void checkValidId(string id)`

   _____

LAB 7-2: WRITING FUNCTIONS THAT REQUIRE A SINGLE PARAMETER

In this lab, you complete a partially written C++ program that includes a function requiring a single parameter. The program prompts the user for an integer. If the integer is divisible by 5, the program calls a function named `divideByFive`. This function displays the message _number_ `divided by 5 is` _result_, where _number_ is the value of `number` and _result_ is the value of `result`. If the number is not divisible by 5, the message `Sorry,` _number_ `is not divisible by 5` is displayed, where _number_ is the value of `number`. The source code file provided for this lab includes the necessary variable declarations and the input statement. Comments are included in the file to help you write the remainder of the program.

1. Open the source code file named `DivideByFive.cpp` using Notepad or the text editor of your choice.

2. Write the C++ statements as indicated by the comments.

3. Save this source code file in a directory of your choice and then make that directory your working directory.

4. Compile the source code file `DivideByFive.cpp`.

5. Execute the program.

WRITING FUNCTIONS THAT REQUIRE MULTIPLE PARAMETERS

In Chapter 7 of _Programming Logic and Design, Fifth Edition,_ you learned that a function often requires more than one parameter in order to accomplish its task. To specify that a function requires multiple parameters, you include a list of data types and local identifiers separated by commas as part of the function's header. To call a function that expects multiple parameters, you list the actual parameters (separated by commas) in the call to the function.

In Figure 7-3, you see the C++ code for a program that includes a function named computeTax that you designed in *Programming Logic and Design, Fifth Edition*. The line numbers are not actually part of the program but are included for reference only.

```
1      // ComputeTax.cpp - This program computes tax given a balance
2      // and a rate
3      // Input:   Interactive
4      // Output:  The balance, tax rate, and computed tax
5
6      #include <iostream>
7      #include <string>
8      void computeTax(double, double);
9      using namespace std;
10
11     int main()
12     {                                           Memory address 1000
13        double balance;
14        double rate;                             Memory address 1008
15
16        cout << "Enter balance: ";
17        cin >> balance;
18        cout << "Enter rate: ";
19        cin >> rate;
20
21        computeTax(balance, rate);
22
23        return 0;
24     } // End of main function              Memory address 9000
25
26     void computeTax(double amount, double rate)
27     {                                           Memory address 9008
28        double tax;
29
30        tax = amount * rate;
31        cout << "Amount: " << amount << " Rate: " << rate << " Tax: "
32              << tax << endl;
33     } // End of computeTax function
```

Figure 7-3 C++ code for ComputeTax program

In the C++ code shown in Figure 7-3, you see that the highlighted call to computeTax on line 21 includes the names of the local variables balance and rate within the parentheses and that they are separated by commas. These are the arguments (actual parameters) that are passed to the computeTax function. You can also see that the computeTax function header on line 26

NOTE
In C++, when you write a function that expects more than one parameter, you must list the parameters separately, even if they have the same data type.

is highlighted and includes two formal parameters, `double amount` and `double rate`, listed within parentheses and separated by commas. The value of the variable named `balance` is passed by value to the `computeTax` function as an actual parameter and is stored in the formal parameter named `amount`. The value of the variable named `rate` is passed by value to the `computeTax` function as an actual parameter and is stored in the formal parameter named `rate`. As illustrated in Figure 7-3, it does not matter that one of the parameters being passed, `rate`, has the same name as the parameter received, `rate`, because they occupy different memory locations.

> **NOTE** There is no limit to the number of arguments you can pass to a function, but when multiple arguments are passed to a function, the call to the function and the function's header must match. This means that the number of arguments/parameters must be the same, their data types must be the same, and the order in which they are listed must be the same.

NOTE
Notice the function declaration on line 8 specifies two parameters (arguments) that are both data type `double`. This agrees with the two `double`s passed to `computeTax` on line 21 and received as two `double`s in the function header on line 26.

Next, you will learn how to write a function that returns a value to the function that called it.

EXERCISE 7-3: WRITING FUNCTIONS THAT REQUIRE MULTIPLE PARAMETERS

In this exercise, you use what you have learned about writing C++ functions that require multiple parameters.

1. Given the following function calls and variable declarations, write the function's header and function declaration:

    a. `string name, date;`

    `printBirthdayInvitation(name, date);`

    _____

    b. `double one_length, two_length;`

    `calculateRectangleArea(one_length, two_length);`

    _____

    c. `int day, month, year;`

    `printNotice(day, month, year);`

    _____

2. Given the following function headers and variable declarations, write a function call:

    a. `string custName = "Smith";`

    `double balance = 54000;`

    `void custInfo(string name, double bal)`

    _____

b. `int val1 = 10, val2 = 20;`

   `void printSum(int num1, int num2)`

---

c. `double salary = 37500, percent = .10;`

   `void increase(double sal, double pcnt)`

LAB 7-3: WRITING FUNCTIONS THAT REQUIRE MULTIPLE PARAMETERS

In this lab, you complete a partially written C++ program that includes a function requiring multiple parameters (arguments). The program prompts the user for an item price and the number of items ordered. If the item's price is less than $5.00, the program should apply a 5% discount; if the item's price is between $5.00 and $9.99, the program should apply a 10% discount; if the item is $10.00 or more, the program should apply a 15% discount. Once the discount is applied, the program should calculate the total price for the number of items purchased and then display the original price, the discount percent, the discounted price, the quantity ordered, and the total price for the items ordered. The source code file provided for this lab includes the variable declarations and the input statements. Comments are included in the file to help you write the remainder of the program.

1. Open the source code file named `DiscountPrices.cpp` using Notepad or the text editor of your choice.

2. Write the C++ statements as indicated by the comments.

3. Save this source code file in a directory of your choice and then make that directory your working directory.

4. Compile the source code file `DiscountPrices.cpp`.

5. Execute the program.

WRITING FUNCTIONS THAT RETURN A VALUE

Thus far in this book, none of the functions you have written (except for the `main` function) return a value. The header for each of these functions includes the keyword `void`, as in

```
void nameAndAddress()
```

indicating that the function does not return a value. However, as a programmer, you will often find that you need to write functions that do return a value. In C++, a function can only return a single value; when you write the code for the function, you must indicate the data type of the value you want to return. This is often referred to as the function's **return type**. The return type can be any of C++'s built-in data types, as well as a class type, such as `string`. You will learn more about classes in Chapter 10 of this book. For now, we will focus on returning values of the built-in types and `string`s.

In Chapter 7 of *Programming Logic and Design, Fifth Edition*, you studied the design for a program that includes a function named `getHoursWorked`. This function is designed to prompt a user for the number of hours an employee has worked, retrieve the value, and then return that value to the location in the program where the function was called. The C++ code that implements this design is shown in Figure 7-4.

```cpp
1    // GrossPay.cpp - This program computes an employee's gross pay.
2    // Input:   Interactive
3    // Output:  The employee's hours worked and their gross pay
4
5    #include <iostream>
6    #include <string>
7    using namespace std;
8    double getHoursWorked();
9
10   int main()
11   {
12      double hours;
13      const double PAY_RATE = 12.00;
14      double gross;
15
16      hours = getHoursWorked();
17      gross = hours * PAY_RATE;
18
19      cout << "Hours worked: " << hours << endl;
20      cout << "Gross pay is: " << gross << endl;
21
22      return 0;
23   } // End of main function
24
25   double getHoursWorked()
26   {
27      double workHours;
28
29      cout << "Please enter hours worked: ";
30      cin >> workHours;
31
32      return workHours;
33   } // End of getHoursWorked function
```

Figure 7-4 C++ code for a program that includes the `getHoursWorked` function

The C++ program shown in Figure 7-4 declares local constants and variables hours, PAY_RATE, and gross on lines 12, 13, and 14 in the main function. The next statement (line 16), shown below, is an assignment statement:

```
hours = getHoursWorked();
```

This assignment statement includes a call to the function named getHoursWorked. As with all assignment statements, the expression on the right side of the assignment operator (=) is evaluated, and then the result is assigned to the variable named on the left side of the assignment operator (=). In this example, the expression on the right is a call to the getHoursWorked function.

When the getHoursWorked function is called, program control is transferred to the function. Notice that the header (line 25) for this function is written as follows:

```
double getHoursWorked()
```

The keyword double is used in the header to specify that a value of data type double is returned by this function. Also, notice on line 8 in the program, the function declaration agrees with the function header. That is, the function declaration specifies that the function returns a double.

A local, double variable named workHours is then declared on line 27. On line 29, the user is asked to enter the number of hours worked, and on line 30 the value is retrieved and stored in the local variable named workHours. The return statement that follows on line 32 returns a copy of the value stored in workHours (data type double) to the location in the calling function where getHoursWorked is called, which is the right side of the assignment statement on line 16.

The value returned to the right side of the assignment statement is then assigned to the variable named hours (data type double) in the main function. Next, the gross pay is calculated on line 17, followed by the cout statements on lines 19 and 20 that display the value of the local variables, hours and gross, which contain the number of hours worked and the calculated gross pay.

You can also use a function's return value directly rather than store it in a variable. The two C++ statements that follow make calls to the same getHoursWorked function shown in Figure 7-4, but in these statements the returned value is used directly in the statement that calculates gross pay and in the statement that prints the returned value:

```
gross = getHoursWorked() * PAY_RATE;
cout << "Hours worked are " << getHoursWorked() << endl;
```

Next, you will learn how to pass an entire array to a function and also how to pass individual elements of an array to a function.

EXERCISE 7-4: WRITING FUNCTIONS THAT RETURN A VALUE

In this exercise, you use what you have learned about writing functions that return a value in C++.

1. Given the following variable declarations and function calls, write the function's header:

   a. ```
   double cost, percent, amount;
   amount = calculateDiscount(cost, percent);
   ```
   _____

   b. ```
   double area, one_length, two_length;
   area = rectArea(one_length, two_length);
   ```
   _____

   c. ```
   string lower_case, upper_case;
   upper_case = changeCase(lower_case);
   ```
   _____

2. Given the following function headers and variable declarations, write a function call:

   a. ```
   int custID = 1234;
   string custName;
   string findName(int custNumber)
   ```
   _____

   b. ```
   int val1 = 10, val2 = 20, sum;
   int add(int num1, int num2)
   ```
   _____

   c. ```
   int number = 3, exponent = 2, result;
   int power(int num, int exp)
   ```
   _____

LAB 7-4: WRITING FUNCTIONS THAT RETURN A VALUE

In this lab, you complete a partially written C++ program that includes a function that returns a value. The program is a simple calculator that prompts the user for two numbers and an operator (+, −, *, or /). The two numbers and the operator are passed to the function where the appropriate arithmetic operation is performed. The result is then returned to the main function where the arithmetic operation and result are displayed. For example, if the user enters 3, 4, and *, the following is displayed:

```
3 * 4 = 12
```

The source code file provided for this lab includes the necessary variable declarations and input and output statements. Comments are included in the file to help you write the remainder of the program.

1. Open the source code file named `Arithmetic.cpp` using Notepad or the text editor of your choice.

2. Write the C++ statements as indicated by the comments.

3. Save this source code file in a directory of your choice and then make that directory your working directory.

4. Compile the source code file `Arithmetic.cpp`.

5. Execute the program.

PASSING AN ARRAY AND AN ARRAY ELEMENT TO A FUNCTION

As a C++ programmer, there are times when you will want to write a function that will perform a task on all of the elements you have stored in an array. For example, in Chapter 7 of *Programming Logic and Design, Fifth Edition*, you saw a design for a program that used a function to quadruple all of the values stored in an array. This design is translated into C++ code in Figure 7-5.

```
1    // PassEntireArray.cpp - This program quadruples the values stored in an array.
2    // Input:   None
3    // Output:  The original values and the quadrupled values
4
5    #include <iostream>
6    #include <string>
7    using namespace std;
8
9    void quadrupleTheValues(int[]);
10   int main()
11   {
12      const int LENGTH = 4;
13      int someNums[] = {10, 12, 22, 35};
14      int x;
15
16      cout << "At beginning of main function. . . " << endl;
17      x = 0;
18      while (x < LENGTH)
19      {
20         cout << someNums[x] << endl;
21         x++;
22      }
```

Figure 7-5 C++ code for `PassEntireArray` program ▶

```
23          quadrupleTheValues(someNums);
24          cout << "At the end of main function. . . " << endl;
25          x = 0;
26          while (x < LENGTH)
27          {
28              cout << someNums[x] << endl;
29              x++;
30          }
31          return 0;
32      } // End of main function
33
34      void quadrupleTheValues(int vals[])
35      {
36          const int LENGTH = 4;
37          int x;
38
39          x = 0;
40          while(x < LENGTH)
41          {
42              cout << " In quadrupleTheValues() function, value is " << vals[x] << endl;
43              x++;
44          }
45          x = 0;
46          while(x < LENGTH)
47          {
48              vals[x] = vals[x] * 4;
49              x++;
50          }
51          x = 0;
52          while(x < LENGTH)
53          {
54              cout << "  After change, value is " << vals[x] << endl;
55              x++;
56          }
57          return;
58      } // End of quadrupleTheValues function
```

Figure 7-5 C++ code for PassEntireArray program (*continued*)

The main function begins on line 10 and proceeds with the declaration and initialization of the constant named LENGTH (line 12) and the array of ints named someNums (line 13), followed by the declaration of the variable named x (line 14), which is used as a loop control variable. The first while loop in the program on lines 18 through 22 is responsible for printing the values stored in the array at the beginning of the program. Next, on line 23, the function named quadrupleTheValues is called. The array named someNums is passed as an argument. Notice that when an entire array is passed to a function, the square brackets and the size are not included. Also note that when you pass an entire array to a function, the beginning memory address of the array is passed by value. This means that instead of a copy of the array being passed, the memory address of the array is passed. Although you cannot change the beginning memory address of the array, this does give the function access to that memory location; the function can then change the values stored in the array if necessary.

Program control is then transferred to the quadrupleTheValues function. The header for the function on line 34 includes one parameter, int vals[]. The syntax for declaring an array as a formal parameter includes the parameter's data type, followed by a local name for the array, followed by empty square brackets. Note that a size is not included within the square brackets.

> **>> NOTE** On line 9, you see the function declaration for the quadrupleTheValues function. The function declaration includes the return type of the function (void), the name of the function (quadrupleTheValues), and the data type of the parameter(s) (int) and empty square brackets ([]) that specify the parameter is an array.

In the quadrupleTheValues function, the first while loop on lines 40 through 44 prints the values stored in the array, and the second while loop on lines 46 through 50 accesses each element in the array, quadruples the value, and then stores the quadrupled values in the array at their same location. The third while loop on lines 52 through 56 prints the changed values now stored in the array. Program control is then returned to the location in the main function where the function was called.

When program control returns to the main function, the next statements to execute (lines 24 through 30) are responsible for printing out the values stored in the array once more. The output from this program is displayed in Figure 7-6.

```
Command Prompt

C:\Users\Jo Ann\C++ Pal\Chapter_7\Student>PassEntireArray
At beginning of main function. . .
10
12
22
35
  In quadrupleTheValues() function, value is 10
  In quadrupleTheValues() function, value is 12
  In quadrupleTheValues() function, value is 22
  In quadrupleTheValues() function, value is 35
  After change, value is 40
  After change, value is 48
  After change, value is 88
  After change, value is 140
At the end of main function. . .
40
48
88
140

C:\Users\Jo Ann\C++ Pal\Chapter_7\Student>
```

Figure 7-6 Output from PassEntireArray program

As shown in Figure 7-6, the array values printed at the beginning of the main function (lines 18 through 22) are the values with which the array was initialized. Next, the quadrupleTheValues function prints the array values (lines 40 through 44) again before they are changed. As shown, the values remain the same as the initialized values. The quadrupleTheValues function then prints the array values again after the values are quadrupled (lines 52 through 56). Finally, after the call to quadrupleTheValues, the main function prints the array values one last time (lines 26 through 30). These are the quadrupled values, indicating that the quadrupleTheValues function has access to the memory location where the array is stored and is able to permanently change the values stored there.

You can also pass a single array element to a function, just as you pass a variable or constant. The following C++ code initializes an array named someNums, declares a variable named newNum, and passes one element of the array to a function named tripleTheNumber. The array element is passed by value in this example, which means a copy of the value stored in the array is passed to the tripleTheNumber function:

```
int someNums[]= {10, 12, 22, 35};
int newNum;
newNum = tripleTheNumber(someNums[1]);
```

The following C++ code includes the header for the function named tripleTheNumber along with the code that triples the value passed to it:

```
int tripleTheNumber(int num)
{
    int result;
    result = num * 3;
    return result;
}
```

Next, you will learn how to pass arguments to a function by reference and by address.

EXERCISE 7-5: PASSING ARRAYS TO FUNCTIONS

In this exercise, you use what you have learned about passing arrays and array elements to functions in C++.

1. Given the following function calls, write the function's header:

   a. int marchBirthdays [] = {3, 12, 13, 22, 27, 31};

   printBirthdayInvitations(marchBirthdays);

   _____

   b. double janSales [] = {100.00, 200.00, 55.00, 230.00};

   double total;

   total = monthlySales(janSales);

   _____

c. ```
double overdue[] = {34.56, 33.22, 65.77, 89.99};
printNotice(overdue[1]);
```

2. Given the following function headers and variable declarations, write a function call:

a. ```
string custNames[] = {"Jones", "Smith", "Brown", "Perez"};
double balances[] = {32.00, 45.00, 76.00, 120.00};
void cust(string name[], double bal[])
```

b. ```
int numbers[] = {1, 4, 6, 8, 3, 7};
int sum;
int printSum(int nums[])
```

3. Given the following function header, write a function call that passes the last value in the array named `salaries`:

a. ```
double salaries[] = {45000, 23000, 35000};
void increase(double sal)
```

LAB 7-5: PASSING ARRAYS TO FUNCTIONS

In this lab, you complete a partially written C++ program that prints student grade reports. The program passes two parallel arrays to a function that prints the grade reports. One array contains `doubles` that represent a student's numeric grade average; the second array contains the names of students stored as `strings`. The function prints the student's name followed by his or her letter grade, as shown below:

```
Name: Maria Frederick - Grade: A
```

In this program, a student earns letter grades as follows:

Numeric Grade	Letter Grade
90 - 99	A
80 - 89	B
70 - 79	C
60 - 69	D
Less than 60	F

The source code file provided for this lab includes the necessary variable declarations. Comments are included in the file to help you write the remainder of the program.

1. Open the source code file named `StudentGrades.cpp` using Notepad or the text editor of your choice.

2. Write the C++ statements as indicated by the comments.

3. Save this source code file in a directory of your choice and then make that directory your working directory.

4. Compile the source code file `StudentGrades.cpp`.

5. Execute the program.

PASSING ARGUMENTS BY REFERENCE AND BY ADDRESS

As a C++ programmer, you will sometimes want to pass one or more arguments to a function and allow the function to permanently change the value of that argument. In the previous section, you learned that when you pass an array to a function, it is actually the beginning memory address of the array that is passed. Because the array's address is passed to a function, the function has access to that memory address and can therefore change the value (or values) that are stored at the memory location.

In C++, there are two techniques you can use to pass the memory address of variables that are not arrays to functions. The two techniques are referred to as **pass by reference** and **pass by address**. We'll begin with a discussion of pass by reference.

PASS BY REFERENCE

Passing an argument to a function by reference allows the called function to access a variable in the calling function. In other words, the called function gains the ability to change the value of a local variable in the calling function. The argument in the called function becomes an **alias** (another name) for the variable in the calling function.

To specify that an argument is passed by reference, you include the & (ampersand) operator in the function declaration and in the function header. You do not use the & operator in the function call. Figure 7-7 shows a C++ program named `IncreaseSalary.cpp` that includes a function named `increase`. The `increase` function calculates an employee's new salary based on a current salary and a percentage that represents an employee's raise.

```
1       // IncreaseSalary.cpp - This program demonstrates pass by reference.
2       // Input:   None
3       // Output:   Beginning salary along with new salary
4       #include <iostream>
5       using namespace std;
6
7       void increase(double, double, double&);
8       int main()
9       {
10         double salary = 50000.00;
11         double raise = .15;
12         double new_salary;
13
14         cout << "Salary is: " << salary << endl;
15
16         // Call the increase function; the variables salary and raise
17         // are passed by value, the variable new_salary is passed by
18         // reference.
19         increase(salary, raise, new_salary);
20
21         cout << "New salary is: " << new_salary << endl;
22         return 0;
23      } // End of main function
24
25      void increase(double amt, double pcnt, double& new_sal)
26      {
27         // Changes the value of new_salary in the main function
28         new_sal = amt * (1 + pcnt);
29         return;
30      }
```

Figure 7-7 Pass by reference example

On line 7 in Figure 7-7, you see the function declaration for the function named increase. The function declaration includes the data types for three arguments that are passed to the increase function. The first two arguments are doubles and the third argument is a reference to a double (double&). The function declaration on line 7 has been shaded in Figure 7-7.

On line 19, you see the function call to the increase function in the main function. The increase function is also shaded so you can easily see that it passes three arguments (salary, raise, and new_salary) that are all local variables declared in the main function.

On line 25, also shaded, you see the header for the increase function that includes three parameters, double amt, double pcnt, and double& new_sal. The first two arguments are passed by value, which means that amt contains a copy of the value stored in salary and pcnt contains a copy of the value stored in raise. The third argument is passed by reference, which means that new_sal is actually an alias for the variable new_salary. Because new_sal is an alias for new_salary, when the value of new_sal is changed on line 28, the value of new_salary, which is declared in the main function, is also changed.

NOTE
In Chapter 3 of this book, you learned that local variables are not available to other functions in the program.

You can compile and execute this program to verify that the `increase` function changes the value of the variable named `new_salary`. The program, named `IncreaseSalary.cpp`, is included with the data files provided with this book.

PASS BY ADDRESS

The second technique you can use to pass the memory address of variables (that are not arrays) to functions is called pass by address. Passing an argument by address allows the called function to change the value of an argument.

Before you can understand passing arguments by address, you must learn about pointers. A **pointer** is a variable that stores a memory address as its value. You are accustomed to using a variable name to directly access a value stored at a memory address associated with a variable. You can also use a pointer variable and the memory address stored in the pointer variable to indirectly access a value stored at a memory address.

The first thing you need to learn in order to use pointers is how to use the address operator. You use the C++ address operator `&` to obtain the memory address associated with a variable. The following C++ code prints the value of a variable named `num` and also uses the address operator `&` to print the memory address associated with the variable named `num`:

```
int num = 5;
cout << "Value of num is: " << num << endl;
cout << "Address of num is: " << &num << endl;
```

As you can see in the preceding, highlighted line of code, the address operator (`&`) is placed before the name of the variable (`num`) to obtain the address of `num`.

Next, you must learn to use the `*` symbol to declare a pointer variable. When you declare a pointer, a specific data type must be explicitly associated with the pointer. The C++ code that follows declares an `int` variable named `age` and `ptr_age` as a pointer to an `int`:

```
int age = 21;
int* ptr_age = &age;
```

Figure 7-8 shows memory after the preceding code executes. The variable named `age` is associated with memory location 2000, where the value 21 is stored. The variable named `ptr_age` is associated with memory location 2004 where the value 2000 (the address of the `int age`) is stored. Because `ptr_age` contains the address of `age`, you can say that `ptr_age` is a pointer to an `int` and that it points to `age`.

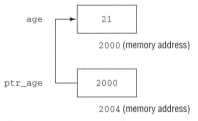

Figure 7-8 Memory contents for `age` and `ptr_age`

The * symbol also serves as the **indirection operator**, which means that it can be used to indirectly access the value to which a pointer points. Because the * symbol is used in many ways in C++, C++ must use context to determine the appropriate meaning. The C++ code that follows shows the use of the * symbol to carry out multiplication, to declare a pointer variable, and to function as the indirection operator:

```
int y = 5;
int x;
int* ptr_x;       // Pointer variable
x = y * 10;       // Multiplication; x is assigned the value 50
ptr_x = &x;       // ptr_x is assigned the memory address of x
cout << *ptr_x;   // Indirection operator; prints 50
```

The C++ program shown in Figure 7-9 shows additional examples in which the * symbol is used to declare a pointer variable and also is used as the indirection operator.

```
1       // PointerPractice.cpp - This program demonstrates pointers.
2       // Input:   None
3       // Output:  Values of variables
4       #include <iostream>
5       using namespace std;
6
7       int main()
8       {
9          int num = 777;
10         int* ptr_num;
11
12         ptr_num = &num;   // Assigns address of num to ptr_num
13
14         cout << "Value of num is: " << num << endl;
15
16         cout << "Value of num is: " << *ptr_num << endl;
17
18         cout << "Address of num is: " << &num << endl;
19
20         cout << "Address of num is: " << ptr_num << endl;
21
22         cout << "Address of ptr_num is: " << &ptr_num << endl;
23
24         return 0;
25      } // End of main function
```

Figure 7-9 C++ program that uses pointer variables and indirection operator

On line 9, the variable num is declared as an int and initialized with the value 777; and on line 10, the variable named ptr_num is declared as a pointer to an int. Line 12 assigns the address of the variable num to ptr_num; and then on line 14, the cout statement prints the value of num by using the name of the variable to directly access its value. The cout statement on line 16 also prints the value of num, but this time the indirection operator is used along with the pointer variable (*ptr_num) to indirectly access the value of num. Next, the address of num is printed on line 18 using the address operator and the name of the variable (&num) to obtain the address of the variable. On line 20, the address of num is printed again, this time using the value stored in the pointer variable ptr_num. The cout statement on line 22 prints the address of ptr_num using the address operator (&ptr_num).

The output of this program is shown is Figure 7-10. Keep in mind that actual memory addresses will vary from one system to another and even from one run of the program to another.

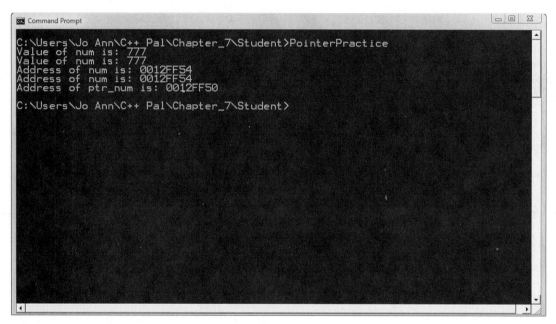

Figure 7-10 Output of PointerPractice program

You can compile and execute this program to see the output values on your system. The program, named PointerPractice.cpp, is included with the data files provided with this book.

To pass an argument(s) to a function using pass by address, the memory address of a local variable(s) in the calling function is passed to the called function. You use the & operator (address operator) when you call the function. The parameter(s) must be declared as a pointer in the function declaration and in the function's header. You use the * symbol to declare the pointer parameter(s). You also must use the * symbol (indirection operator) to dereference the pointer(s) in the body of the function. **Dereferencing** a pointer means that you use the indirection operator to indirectly gain access to the value of a variable.

The C++ program shown in Figure 7-11 illustrates the use of pass by address.

```
1      // PassByAddress.cpp - This program demonstrates pass by address.
2      // Input:  None
3      // Output:  Values of variables
4      #include <iostream>
5      using namespace std;
6
7      void swap(int*, int*);
8
9      int main()
10     {
11        int num1 = 5;
12        int num2 = 10;
13
14        cout << "Value of num1 is: " << num1 << endl;
15
16        cout << "Value of num2 is: " << num2 << endl;
17
18        swap(&num1,  &num2);
19
20        cout << "Value of num1 is: " << num1 << endl;
21
22        cout << "Value of num2 is: " << num2 << endl;
23
24        return 0;
25     } // End of main function
26
27     void swap(int* val1, int* val2)
28     {
29        int temp;
30        temp = *val1;
31        *val1 = *val2;
32        *val2 = temp;
33     }
```

Figure 7-11 C++ program that uses pass by address

The function declaration for the swap function is shown on line 7. Notice the swap function does not return a value (void) and specifies two parameters, both pointers to ints (int*, int*).

In the main function on lines 11 and 12, two int variables, num1 and num2, are declared and initialized to the values 5 and 10, respectively. Both of these variables, num1 and num2, are local to the main function, which means that the swap function does not have direct access to them. On lines 14 and 16, the values of num1 (5) and num2 (10) are printed.

Next, on line 18, the swap function is called, passing the address of num1 (&num1) and the address of num2 (&num2) to the function. Because the memory addresses of num1 and num2 are passed, the swap function has access to the values stored at those memory addresses and will be able to change the values stored there.

Program control is now passed to the swap function. The header for the swap function on line 27 specifies that the function does not return a value and accepts two parameters, val1 and val2. The two parameters are declared as pointers to ints (int* val1, int* val2). The parameter val1 contains the address of num1 and the parameter val2 contains the address of num2. On line 29, the int variable named temp is declared. Because val1 and val2 are both pointers, the indirection operator (*) is used on lines 30, 31, and 32 to gain access to the values stored in memory that are pointed to by val1 and val2. On line 30, the value pointed to by val1 (the value of num1) is accessed indirectly and then assigned to temp. On line 31, the value pointed to by val2 (the value of num2) is accessed indirectly then assigned to what val1 points to, which is num1. This assignment statement changes the value of num1 in the main function. Line 32 assigns the value stored in temp to what val2 points to, which is num2. This assignment changes the value of num2 in the main function.

When the swap function returns control to the main function, the values of num1 and num2 are displayed again on lines 20 and 22. This time, the value of num1 is 10 and the value of num2 is 5, illustrating that the local variables num1 and num2 have been changed by the swap function.

You can compile and execute this program to see the output values on your system. The program, named PassByAddress.cpp, is included with the data files provided with this book.

Next, you will learn what it means to overload a function and how to accomplish overloading functions in C++.

EXERCISE 7-6: PASS BY REFERENCE AND PASS BY ADDRESS

In this exercise, you use what you have learned about passing arguments by reference and by address to functions in C++.

1. Given the following variable and function declarations, write the function call and the function's header:

   a. double price = 22.95, increase = .10;

   void changePrice(double&, double);

   _____

   _____

   b. double price = 22.95, increase = .10;

   void changePrice(double* , double);

   _____

   _____

c.
```
int age = 23;
void changeAge(int&);
```

_____

_____

d.
```
int age = 23;
void changeAge(int*);
```

_____

_____

2. Given the following function headers and variable declarations, write a function call:

a.
```
custNames[] = {"Perez", "Smith", "Patel", "Shaw"};
balances[] = {34.00, 21.00, 45.50, 67.00};
void cust(string name[], double bal[])
```

_____

b.
```
int values[] = {1, 77, 89, 321, -2, 34};
void printSum(int nums[])
```

_____

LAB 7-6: PASS BY REFERENCE AND PASS BY ADDRESS

In this lab, you complete a partially written C++ program that includes a function named addNumbers that adds three int values to find their sum. Four ints should be passed to the addNumbers function, the three numbers to be added (num1, num2, and num3) should be passed by value, and another int (sum) to hold the sum of the three numbers should be passed by reference, enabling the addNumbers function to change its value.

The source code file provided for this lab includes the necessary variable declarations and input and output statements. Comments are included in the file to help you write the remainder of the program.

1. Open the source code file named AddThree.cpp using Notepad or the text editor of your choice.

2. Write the addNumbers function, the function declaration, and the function call as indicated by the comments.

3. Save this source code file in a directory of your choice and then make that directory your working directory.

4. Compile the source code file AddThree.cpp.

5. Execute the program.

6. Rewrite the `addNumbers` function to pass the three numbers (`num1`, `num2`, and `num3`) by value and pass `sum` by address.

7. Save this program as `AddThree2.cpp`.

8. Compile `AddThree2.cpp`.

9. Execute the program. Both programs (`AddThree.cpp` and `AddThree2.cpp`) should generate the same output.

OVERLOADING FUNCTIONS

You can overload functions by giving the same name and different parameter lists to multiple functions. Overloading a function is useful when you need to perform the same action on different types of inputs. For example, you may want to write multiple versions of an `add` function—one that can add two `int`s, another that can add two `double`s, another that can add three `int`s, and another that can add two `int`s and a `double`, to name just a few different types of inputs. Overloaded functions have the same name but require a different number of arguments, or the arguments must be of different data types. C++ figures out which function to call based on the function's name and its arguments, the combination of which is known as the function's **signature**. It's important to understand that the signature of a function consists of the function's name and its argument list; it does not include the function's return type.

Overloading functions allows a C++ programmer to choose meaningful names for functions and also permits the use of polymorphic code. **Polymorphic** code is code that acts appropriately depending on the context. (The word "polymorphic" is derived from the Greek words "poly", meaning "many," and "morph", meaning "form.") Polymorphic functions in C++ can take many forms. You will learn more about polymorphism in other C++ courses, when you learn more about object-oriented programming. For now, you can use overloading to write functions that perform the same task but with different data types.

In Chapter 7 of *Programming Logic and Design, Fifth Edition,* you studied the design for an overloaded function named `printBill`; one version includes a numeric parameter, a second version includes two numeric parameters, a third version includes a numeric parameter and a string parameter, and a fourth version includes two numeric parameters and a string parameter. All versions of the `printBill` function have the same name with a different signature; therefore, it is an overloaded function. In Figure 7-12 you see a C++ program that includes the four versions of the `printBill` function.

```
1     // Overloaded.cpp - This program illustrates overloaded methods.
2     // Input:  None
3     // Output:  Bill printed in various ways
4
5     #include <iostream>
6     #include <string>
7     using namespace std;
8
9     void printBill(double);
10    void printBill(double, double);
11    void printBill(double, string);
12    void printBill(double, double, string);
13
14    int main()
15    {
16       double bal = 250.00, discountRate = .05;
17       string msg = "Due in 10 days.";
18
19       printBill(bal);                        // Call version #1
20       printBill(bal, discountRate);          // Call version #2
21       printBill(bal, msg);                   // Call version #3
22       printBill(bal, discountRate, msg);     // Call version #4
23
24       return 0;
25    } // End of main function
26
27    // printBill function #1
28    void printBill(double balance)
29    {
30       cout << "Thank you for your order." << endl;
31       cout << "Please remit " << balance << endl;
32    } // End of printBill #1 function
33
34    // printBill function #2
35    void printBill(double balance, double discount)
36    {
37       double newBal;
38       newBal = balance - (balance * discount);
39       cout << "Thank you for your order." << endl;
40       cout << "Please remit " << newBal << endl;
41    } // End of printBill #2 function
42
43    // printBill function #3
44    void printBill(double balance, string message)
45    {
46       cout << "Thank you for your order." << endl;
47       cout << message << endl;
48       cout << "Please remit " << balance << endl;
49    } // End of printBill #3 function
```

Figure 7-12 Program that uses overloaded printBill functions ▶

```
50
51      // printBill function #4
52      void printBill(double balance, double discount, string message)
53      {
54          double  newBal;
55          newBal = balance - (balance * discount);
56          cout << "Thank you for your order." << endl;
57          cout << message << endl;
58          cout << "Please remit " << newBal << endl;
59      } // End of printBill #4 function
```

Figure 7-12 Program that uses overloaded `printBill` functions (*continued*)

On line 19, the first call to the `printBill` function passes one argument, the variable named `bal`, which is declared as a `double`. This causes the run-time system to find and execute the `printBill` function that is written to accept one `double` as an argument (line 28). The third call to the `printBill` function (line 21) passes two arguments, a `double` and a `string`. This causes the run-time system to find and execute the `printBill` function that is written to accept a `double` and a `string` as arguments (line 44). You can compile and execute this program if you would like to verify that a different version of the `printBill` function is called when a different number of arguments are passed or arguments of different data types are passed. The program, named `Overloaded.cpp`, is included with the data files provided with this book.

Next, you will learn about using functions that you do not have to write yourself because they are built into the C++ programming language.

EXERCISE 7-7: OVERLOADING FUNCTIONS

In this exercise, you use what you have learned about overloading functions.

1. In Figure 7-13, which function header would the following function calls match? Use a line number as your answer.

```
1      // Method headers
2      int sum(int num1, int num2)
3      int sum(int num2, int num2, int num3)
4      double sum(double num1, double num2)
5      // Variable declarations
6      double number1 = 1.0, ans1;
7      int number2 = 5, ans2;
```

Figure 7-13 Function headers and variable declarations

a. `ans2 = sum(2,5);`

_____

b. `ans1 = sum(number1, number1);`

_____

```
c. ans1 = sum(2.0, 5.0);
```

_____

```
d. ans2 = sum(2, 4, number2);
```

_____

```
e. ans2 = sum(3, 5, 7);
```

_____

LAB 7-7: OVERLOADING FUNCTIONS

In this lab, you complete a partially written C++ program that includes overloaded functions. The program is written to check if a student provided correct answers on a test. The test includes three questions. One question requires an `int` for the answer, one question requires a `string` for the answer, and another question requires a `bool` for the answer. The source code file provided for this lab includes variable declarations that are initialized with a student's answers. It also includes the necessary output statements. You must write three overloaded functions named `checkQuestion`. One of the functions should accept an `int` argument that represents the student's `int` answer, one should accept a `string` argument that represents the student's `string` answer, and one should accept a `bool` argument that represents the student's `bool` answer. In the functions, you should test for correct answers and return the `string` value "Correct" or "Incorrect". The correct `int` answer is 3, the correct `string` answer is "George Washington", and the correct `bool` answer is true. Comments are included in the file to help you write the remainder of the program.

1. Open the source code file named `CheckAnswer.cpp` using Notepad or the text editor of your choice.

2. Write the C++ statements as indicated by the comments.

3. Save this source code file in a directory of your choice and then make that directory your working directory.

4. Compile the source code file `CheckAnswer.cpp`.

5. Execute the program.

USING C++ BUILT-IN FUNCTIONS

Until now, you have been told that you do not know enough about the C++ programming language to be able to control the number of places displayed after the decimal point when you print a value of data type `double`. There are actually several ways to control the number of places displayed after a decimal point. In this section, we will look at one approach: using a manipulator named `setprecision`. A **manipulator** is a special C++ function that can control (manipulate) how data is displayed. Throughout this book, you have been using the `endl` manipulator to display a new line character.

In the C++ program that follows, you see how the setprecision manipulator is used to control the number of digits displayed.

```cpp
#include <iostream>
#include <iomanip>
using namespace std;
int main()
{
    double value = 3.14159;
    cout << value << endl;
    cout << setprecision(1) << value << endl;
    cout << setprecision(2) << value << endl;
    cout << setprecision(3) << value << endl;
    cout << setprecision(4) << value << endl;
    cout << setprecision(5) << value << endl;
    cout << setprecision(6) << value << endl;
    return 0;
}
```

In the preceding code sample, setprecision is a manipulator that controls how the floating point value should be formatted. The setprecision manipulator requires one integer argument that specifies the maximum number of digits to display including both those before and those after the decimal point. For example, the C++ code

```cpp
double value = 3.14159;
cout << setprecision(3) << value << endl;
```

produces the following output: 3.14.

You can compile and execute this program to see how the number of digits changes with different integer arguments provided to setprecision. The program, named Precision.cpp, is included with the data files provided with this book.

As you continue to learn more about C++, you will be introduced to many more built-in functions that you can use in your programs.

EXERCISE 7-8: USING C++'S BUILT-IN FUNCTIONS

In this exercise, you use a browser, such as Google, to find information about a built-in function that belongs to the C++ function library and then answer the following questions:

1. What does the pow function do?

   _____

2. What data type does the pow function return?

   _____

3. Is the pow function overloaded? How do you know?

   _____

4. How many arguments does the `pow` function require?

_____

5. What is the data type of the argument(s)?

_____

6. What is the value of the variable named `result`?

```
result = pow(3,6);
```

_____

7. What is the value of the variable named `result`?

```
result = pow(12, 3);
```

_____

LAB 7-8: USING C++'S BUILT-IN FUNCTIONS

In this lab, you complete a partially written C++ program that includes built-in functions that convert characters stored in a character array to all uppercase or all lowercase. The program prompts the user to enter nine characters. For each character in the array, you call the built-in functions `tolower` and `toupper`. Both of these functions return a character with the character changed to uppercase or lowercase. Here is an example:

```
char sample1 = 'A';
char sample2 = 'a';
char result1, result2;
result1 = tolower(sample1);
result2 = toupper(sample2);
```

The source code file provided for this lab includes the necessary variable declarations and the necessary input and output statements. Comments are included in the file to help you write the remainder of the program.

1. Open the source code file named `ChangeCase.cpp` using Notepad or the text editor of your choice.

2. Write the C++ statements as indicated by the comments.

3. Save this source code file in a directory of your choice and then make that directory your working directory.

4. Compile the source code file `ChangeCase.cpp`.

5. Execute the program with the following data:

```
lowercase
```

```
UPPERCASE
```

CHAPTER

8

WRITING CONTROL BREAK PROGRAMS

After studyıng thıs chapter, you wıll be able to:

Understand single-level control break programs
Understand how to accumulate totals in single-level
    control break programs
Use multiple-level control breaks in a C++ program

In this chapter, you will learn how to write a single-level control break program that accumulates totals. You will also learn how to write programs that employ multiple-level control breaks. You should do the exercises and labs in this chapter only after you have finished Chapter 8 of your text, *Programming Logic and Design, Fifth Edition*, by Joyce Farrell.

ACCUMULATING TOTALS IN SINGLE-LEVEL CONTROL BREAK PROGRAMS

A **single-level control break** program causes a break in the logic based on the value of a single variable. In Chapter 8 of *Programming Logic and Design, Fifth Edition*, you learned about techniques you can employ to implement a single-level control break program. Be sure you understand these techniques before you continue on with this chapter. The Bookstore program described in Chapter 8 of *Programming Logic and Design, Fifth Edition*, is an example of a single-level control break program. The Bookstore program reads a record for each book that a bookstore sells, keeps a count of the number of books in each category, and keeps a grand total of all of the books carried by the bookstore. As shown in Figure 8-1, the report generated by this program includes book titles, a count of the number of books in each category, and a count of all books. The output lines that make up the report are shown interspersed with the program's input. Once you learn to perform file input in the next chapter, the input lines will no longer appear.

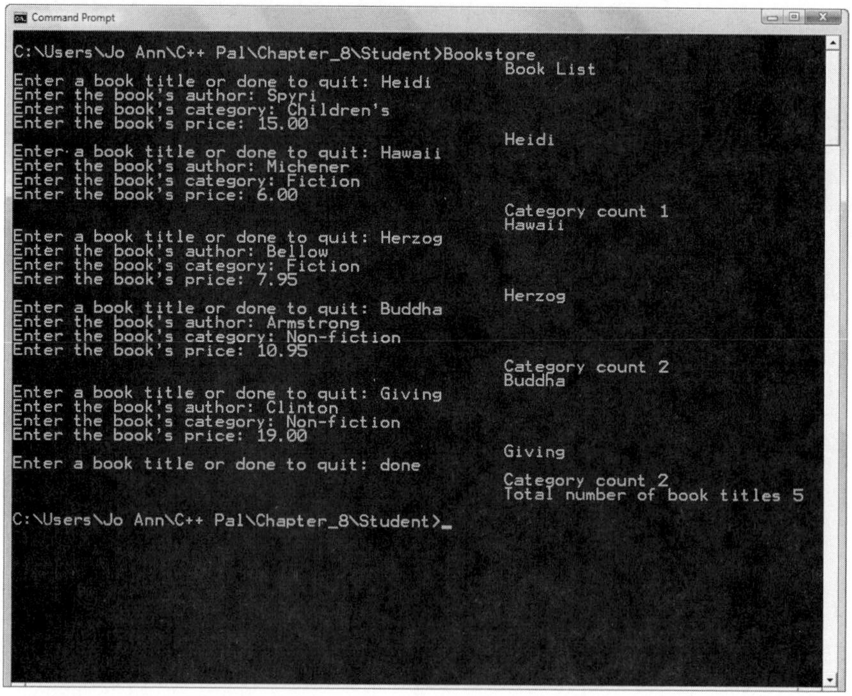

Figure 8-1 Bookstore program report

Each book record is made up of the following fields: Book Title, Author, Price, and Book Category. Note the following example records, each made up of four lines:

```
Heidi
Spyri
15.00
Children's

------------------------------------

Hawaii
Michener
6.95
Fiction
```

Input records for a control break program are usually stored in a data file on a storage device, such as a disk, and the records are sorted according to a predetermined control break variable. For example, the control break variable for this program is category, so the input records would be sorted according to category. You have not yet learned about reading data from an input file, so for this program the input will continue to be interactive. You will learn about reading input data from a file in the next chapter.

Figure 8-2 includes the pseudocode for the Bookstore program and Figure 8-3 includes the C++ code that implements the program.

```
start
   string title
   string author
   string category
   num price
   string HEADING = "BOOK LIST"
   string FOOTER = "Total number of book titles "
   string CATEGORY_FOOTER = "Category count "
   num grandTotal = 0
   string prevCategory
   num categoryTotal = 0
   print HEADING
   get title, author, category, price
   prevCategory = category
   while not eof
      if category not = prevCategory then
         grandTotal = categoryChange(categoryTotal, grandTotal)
         categoryTotal = 0
         prevCategory = category
      endif
      categoryTotal = categoryTotal + 1
      print title
      get title, author, category, price
```

Figure 8-2 Bookstore program pseudocode ▶

```
      endwhile
      print CATEGORY_FOOTER, categoryTotal
      grandTotal = grandTotal + categoryTotal
      print FOOTER, grandTotal
   stop

   num categoryChange(num categoryTotal, num grandTotal)
      string CATEGORY_FOOTER = "Category count "
      print CATEGORY_FOOTER, categoryTotal
      grandTotal = grandTotal + categoryTotal
   return grandTotal
```

Figure 8-2 Bookstore program pseudocode (*continued*)

```
1      // Bookstore.cpp - This program creates a report that lists
2      // all of the books carried by a bookstore with a count
3      // for each book category and a grand total.
4      // Input:   Interactive.
5      // Output:  Report
6      #include <iostream>
7      #include <string>
8      using namespace std;
9      int categoryChange(int, int);
10     int main()
11     {
12        double price;
13        string title, author, category;
14        const string HEADING = "Book List";
15        const string FOOTER = "Total number of book titles ";
16        const string CATEGORY_FOOTER = "Category count ";
17        const string SENTINEL = "done";
18        int grandTotal = 0;
19        string prevCategory = "";
20        int categoryTotal = 0;
21        bool notDone = true;
22
23        cout << "\t\t\t\t\t\t" << HEADING << endl;
24        cout << "Enter a book title or done to quit: ";
25        cin >> title;
26        if(title == SENTINEL)
27        {
28           notDone = false;
29        }
```

Figure 8-3 Bookstore program written in C++   ▶

```
30        else
31        {
32            cout << "Enter the book's author: ";
33            cin >> author;
34            cout << "Enter the book's category: ";
35            cin >> category;
36            cout << "Enter the book's price: ";
37            cin >> price;
38            prevCategory = category;
39        }
40        while(notDone == true)
41        {
42            if(category != prevCategory)
43            {
44                grandTotal = categoryChange(categoryTotal, grandTotal);
45                categoryTotal = 0;
46                prevCategory = category;
47            }
48            categoryTotal++;
49            cout << "\t\t\t\t\t\t" << title << endl;
50            cout << "Enter a book title or done to quit: ";
51            cin >> title;
52            if(title == SENTINEL)
53            {
54                notDone = false;
55            }
56            else
57            {
58                cout << "Enter the book's author: ";
59                cin >> author;
60                cout << "Enter the book's category: ";
61                cin >> category;
62                cout << "Enter the book's price: ";
63                cin >> price;
64            }
65        }
66        cout << "\t\t\t\t\t\t" << CATEGORY_FOOTER << categoryTotal << endl;
67        grandTotal += categoryTotal;
68        cout << "\t\t\t\t\t\t" << FOOTER << grandTotal << endl;
69        return 0;
70   } // End of main function
71
72   // categoryChange function
73   int categoryChange(int categoryTotal, int grandTotal)
74   {
75        const string CATEGORY_FOOTER = "Category count ";
76
77        cout << "\t\t\t\t\t\t" << CATEGORY_FOOTER << categoryTotal << endl;
78        grandTotal += categoryTotal;
79        return(grandTotal);
80   } // End of categoryChange function
```

Figure 8-3 Bookstore program written in C++ (*continued*)

As you can see in Figure 8-3, the C++ program begins on line 1 with comments that describe what the program does. (Remember, the line numbers shown in this program are not part of the C++ code. They are included for reference only.) The program also includes comments that describe the program's input and output. Next come two preprocessor directives on lines 6 and 7, the using namespace std; statement on line 8, and the function declaration for the categoryChange function on line 9. Notice that the categoryChange function returns an int and accepts two ints as arguments. The C++ code that begins the main function is on line 10.

Within the main function, lines 12 through 23 declare variables and constants, initialize them when appropriate, and then print the heading for the report. The cout statement on line 23 includes the string "\t\t\t\t\t\t" as part of the output it generates. In C++, "\t" represents a tab character. Thus, the string "\t\t\t\t\t\t" represents a string of six tab characters. Including this string in a cout statement forces lines to be indented six tabs. That means the statement cout << "\t\t\t\t\t\t" << HEADING << endl; indents six times before printing the constant HEADING and a newline character.

The next step is to perform a priming read to get the first input record, which consists of a single book's title, author, price, and category. You learned about performing a priming read in Chapter 3 of this book and in Chapter 2 of *Programming Logic and Design, Fifth Edition*.

Notice that the C++ code in the priming read (lines 24 and 25) is a little different than the pseudocode. When the user is asked to input a book's title, he or she is also instructed to enter the word "done" after inputting records. Also, an if statement is used on line 26 to test if the user entered a book's title or the word "done". If the user is done entering records, the result of this test will be true, causing the bool value false to be assigned to the variable named notDone on line 28 and the remainder of the input statements asking for the author, category, and price will not execute. The bool variable named notDone is used later in the program to control the while loop. If the user is not finished entering records, he or she is prompted to enter the rest of the book's data: the author, category, and price on lines 32 through 37. On line 38, the value of the current book's category (category) is assigned to the variable named prevCategory. The variable category serves as the control break variable.

> **»NOTE** For the sake of simplicity, this example program only allows the user to enter single-word book titles and the author's last name. This simplification is designed to keep the input straightforward. Inputting strings that contain multiple words involves learning some intricacies of C++ that you will be introduced to when you take a C++ course.

Next comes the while loop (line 40), which continues to execute as long as the value of the bool variable notDone is true. Within the body of the while loop, the if statement tests the control break variable category on line 42. The if statement's job is to determine if the record the user is currently working with has the same category as the previous record's category. If it does not, this indicates the beginning of a new category. As a result, the program calls the categoryChange function (line 44), which is the control break function. Notice, the return value of this function is assigned to the variable named `grandTotal` and that two arguments, `categoryTotal` and `grandTotal`, are passed to the function. The `categoryChange` function, which begins on line 73, does the following:

1. Prints six tab characters followed by the value of the local constant named `CATEGORY_FOOTER` and the value of `categoryTotal`, which contains the count of books in the current category (line 77).

2. Adds the value of `categoryTotal` to `grandTotal`, which is the variable used to accumulate the total of all books (line 78).

3. Returns the value of `grandTotal` (line 79) to the location in the `main` function where the `categoryChange` function was called (line 44).

When the `categoryChange` function is finished executing, the following occurs:

» The function's return value is assigned to the variable named `grandTotal` on line 44, thereby updating the total number of books.

» The variable named `categoryTotal` is assigned the value 0 to prepare for the beginning of a new category (line 45).

» The previous category variable, `prevCategory`, is assigned the value of the current category (`category`) to prepare for a new category (line 46).

The next statement to execute (line 48) adds 1 to the category counter variable named `categoryTotal`. It is important to understand that this statement executes both when a category changes and when a category does not change. Finally, lines 49 through 64 print the title of the current book and then get the next book's input data using the same technique as in the priming read. The condition in the `while` loop on line 40 is then tested again, causing the loop to continue executing until the user enters the word "`done`" instead of a book's title.

When the `while` loop is exited, the last section of the program executes. This consists of:

» Printing six tab characters followed by the value of the local constant named `CATEGORY_FOOTER` along with the value of `categoryTotal` (which is the total of the last category input by the user) on line 66

» Adding the value of `categoryTotal` to the variable named `grandTotal` on line 67

» Printing six tab characters followed by the value of the local constant named `FOOTER` along with the value of `grandTotal`, which now contains the total of all books carried by the bookstore on line 68

Now that you have seen a single-level control break program, in the next section you will learn how to write a multiple-level control break C++ program.

EXERCISE 8-1: ACCUMULATING TOTALS IN SINGLE-LEVEL CONTROL BREAK PROGRAMS

In this exercise, you use what you have learned about accumulating totals in a single-level control break program to answer specific questions. First, study the C++ code that follows:

```
if(itemNum != oldItemNum)
{
    cout << "Item Number " << oldItemNum << endl;
    totalItems = itemNum;
    oldItemNum = itemNum;
}
```

1. What is the control break variable?

2. The value of the control break variable should never be changed. True or false?

3. Is totalItems being calculated correctly?

   If not, how can you fix the code?

4. In a control break program, it doesn't matter if the records in the input file are in a specified order. True or false?

LAB 8-1: ACCUMULATING TOTALS IN SINGLE-LEVEL CONTROL BREAK PROGRAMS

In this lab, you use what you have learned about accumulating totals in a single-level control break program to complete a C++ program. The program should produce a report for a fast food restaurant owner to help her keep track of hours worked by her part-time employees. The report should include the day of the week and the number of hours worked for each employee for each day of the week, the total hours for the day of the week, and at the end of the week, the total hours worked that week. The report should look similar to the one shown in Figure 8-4.

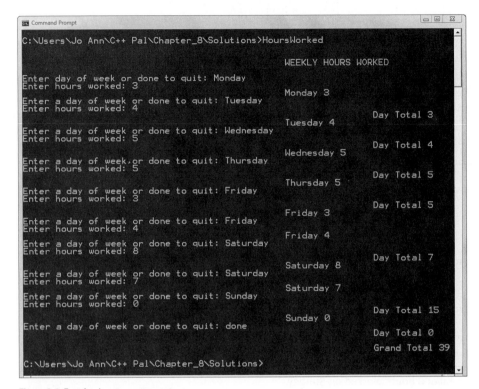

Figure 8-4 Fast food restaurant report

The student file provided for this lab includes the necessary variable declarations and input and output statements. You need to implement the code that recognizes when a control break should occur. You also need to complete the control break function. Be sure to accumulate the daily totals and the grand total for all days in the week. Comments in the code tell you where to write your code. You can use the Bookstore program in this chapter as a guide for this new program.

1. Open the source code file named `HoursWorked.cpp` using Notepad or the text editor of your choice.

2. Study the prewritten code to understand what has already been done.

3. Write the control break code in the `main` function.

4. Write the `dayChange` control break function.

5. Save this source code file in a directory of your choice and then make that directory your working directory.

6. Compile the source code file `HoursWorked.cpp`.

7. Execute the program.

Execute this program using the following input values:

Monday – 3 hours (employee 1)

Tuesday – 4 hours (employee 1)

Wednesday – 5 hours (employee 1)

Thursday – 5 hours (employee 1)

Friday – 3 hours (employee 1), 4 hours (employee 2)

Saturday – 7 hours (employee 1), 8 hours (employee 2)

Sunday – 0 hours

The program results should include:

A total of 3 hours worked on Monday.

A total of 4 hours worked on Tuesday.

A total of 5 hours worked on Wednesday.

A total of 5 hours worked on Thursday.

A total of 7 hours worked on Friday.

A total of 15 hours worked on Saturday.

A total of 0 hours worked on Sunday.

A grand total of 39 hours worked for the week.

MULTIPLE-LEVEL CONTROL BREAK PROGRAMS

In Chapter 8 of *Programming Logic and Design, Fifth Edition*, you learned how to implement a multiple-level control break program. Make sure you understand this material before you continue with this chapter.

A multiple-level control break program performs special processing in response to more than one condition. In this section, you will study a modified version of the Bookstore program, which makes use of a multiple-level control break. In this version, the program generates a report that prints a summary of books sold in each city and each state. To generate this type of summary report, a control break must occur when the name of the city changes. A second control break must occur when the name of the state changes.

You learned that for a single-level control break program, the input must be sorted according to a predetermined control break variable; similarly, the input for a multiple-level control break program must be sorted by multiple control break variables. In this case, the input must be sorted by city within state.

Figure 8-5 contains the pseudocode for the modified Bookstore program that was developed in Chapter 8 of *Programming Logic and Design, Fifth Edition*, and Figure 8-6 contains the C++ code for that design.

```
start
   string title
   num price
   string HEADING = "BOOK LIST"
   string FOOTER = "Total number of book titles "
   num GRAND = 2
   num STATE = 1
   num CITY = 0
   num total[3] = 0, 0, 0
   string prev[2]

   print HEADING
   get title, price, city, state
   prev[STATE] = state
   prev[CITY] = city
   while not eof
      if state not = prev[STATE] then
         stateBreak(total, prev, state, city)
      else
         if city not = prev[CITY] then
            cityBreak(total, prev, city)
         endif
      endif
      total[CITY] = total[CITY] + 1
      get title, price, city, state
   endwhile
   stateBreak(total, prev, state, city)
   print FOOTER, total[GRAND]
stop
void cityBreak(num total[], num prev[], string city)
   num GRAND = 2
   num STATE = 1
   num CITY = 0
   print prev[CITY], total[CITY]
   total [STATE] = total [STATE] + total [CITY]
   total[CITY] = 0
   prev[CITY] = city
return
```

Figure 8-5 Modified Bookstore program pseudocode ▶

```
void stateBreak(num total[], num prev[], string state, string city)
   num GRAND = 2
   num STATE = 1
   num CITY = 0
   string EXPLANATION = "Total for "
   cityBreak(total, prev, city)
   print EXPLANATION, prev[STATE], total[STATE]
   total[GRAND] = total[GRAND] + total[STATE]
   total[STATE] = 0
   prev[STATE] = state
return
```

Figure 8-5 Modified Bookstore program pseudocode (*continued*)

```
1    // Bookstore2.cpp - This program creates a report that lists
2    // all of the books sold in each city and each state.
3    // Input:   Interactive
4    // Output:  Report
5    #include <iostream>
6    #include <string>
7    using namespace std;
8    void cityBreak(int total[], string prev[], string city);
9    void stateBreak(int total[], string prev[], string state, string city);
10   int main()
11   {
12      double price;
13      string title, city = "", state = "";
14      const string HEADING = "Book List";
15      const string FOOTER = "Total number of book titles ";
16      const string SENTINEL = "done";
17      const int GRAND = 2;
18      const int STATE = 1;
19      const int CITY = 0;
20      int total[] = {0, 0, 0};
21      string prev[2];
22      bool notDone = true;
23
24      cout << "\t\t\t\t\t\t" << HEADING << endl;
25      cout << "Enter a book title or done to quit: ";
26      cin >> title;
27      if(title == SENTINEL)
28      {
29         notDone = false;
30      }
```

Figure 8-6 Modified Bookstore program written in C++ ▶

152

```
31        else
32        {
33           cout << "Enter the book's price: ";
34           cin >> price;
35           cout << "Enter the city: ";
36           cin >> city;
37           cout << "Enter the state: ";
38           cin >> state;
39           prev[STATE] = state;
40           prev[CITY] = city;
41        }
42        while(notDone == true)
43        {
44           if(state != prev[STATE])
45              stateBreak(total, prev, state, city);
46           else if(city != prev[CITY])
47              cityBreak(total, prev, city);
48           total[CITY] ++;
49           cout << "Enter a book title or done to quit: ";
50           cin >> title;
51           if(title == SENTINEL)
52           {
53              notDone = false;
54           }
55           else
56           {
57              cout << "Enter the book's price: ";
58              cin >> price;
59              cout << "Enter the city: ";
60              cin >> city;
61              cout << "Enter the state: ";
62              cin >> state;
63           }
64        }
65        stateBreak(total, prev, state, city);
66        cout << "\t\t\t\t\t\t" << FOOTER << total[GRAND] << endl;
67        return 0;
68     } // End of main function
69
70     void cityBreak(int total[], string prev[], string city)
71     {
72        const int GRAND = 2;
73        const int STATE = 1;
74        const int CITY = 0;
75
76        cout << "\t\t\t\t\t\t" << prev[CITY] << " " << total[CITY] << endl;
77        total[STATE] += total[CITY];
78        total[CITY] = 0;
79        prev[CITY] = city;
80     } // End of cityBreak function
```

Figure 8-6 Modified Bookstore program written in C++ (*continued*) ▶

```
81
82    void stateBreak(int total[], string prev[], string state, string city)
83    {
84        const int GRAND = 2;
85        const int STATE = 1;
86        const int CITY = 0;
87        const string EXPLANATION = "Total for ";
88
89        cityBreak(total, prev, city);
90        cout << "\t\t\t\t\t\t" << EXPLANATION << prev[STATE]
               << " " <<    total[STATE] << endl;
91        total[GRAND] += total[STATE];
92        total[STATE] = 0;
93        prev[STATE] = state;
94    } // End of stateBreak function
```

Figure 8-6 Modified Bookstore program written in C++ (*continued*)

As you can see in Figure 8-6, the C++ program begins with comments (lines 1 through 4) that describe: 1) what the program does; and 2) the program's input and output. Next comes two preprocessor directives on lines 5 and 6, the using namespace std; statement on line 7, and the function declaration for the cityBreak and stateBreak functions on lines 8 and 9. Notice that the cityBreak function returns nothing (void) and accepts three arguments: an int array, a string array, and a string. Also, notice that the stateBreak function returns nothing (void) and accepts four arguments: an int array, a string array, and two strings. The C++ code that begins the main function is on line 10.

Within the main function on lines 12 through 24, variables and constants are declared and initialized when appropriate, and the heading for the report is printed. Notice that two of the variables declared are arrays: an array of ints named total and an array of strings named prev. The total array is used to store a city total, a state total, and a grand total, and the prev array is used to store the name of the previous city and state. The constants CITY, STATE, and GRAND are used as index values to access an element of the total array, and the constants CITY and STATE are used to access the name of the previous city and previous state stored in the prev array. The variables named city and state are used as control break variables to process the two control breaks in this program.

Using the same technique that is employed in the original Bookstore program, a priming read (lines 25 through 38) gets the first input record. In this version of the program, an input record now consists of a single book's title, price, city, and state. If the user is not finished inputting records, the program also assigns the value of state to prev[STATE] and the value of city to prev[CITY] on lines 39 and 40.

The while loop on line 42 continues to execute as long as the value of the bool variable notDone is true. Within the body of the while loop, the if statement tests the first control break variable, state (line 44), to determine if the record currently being processed has the same state as the previous record. If it does not, we know that a new state has been encountered. In that case, the program calls the stateBreak function (line 45), which is one of the control break functions. Notice that four arguments—`total`, `prev`, `state`, and `city`—are passed to this function. As you learned in Chapter 7 of this book, the beginning addresses of the two arrays `total` and `prev` are passed by value, giving the function access to the memory locations and therefore the ability to change the values stored in the arrays. The arguments `state` and `city` are both `string`s and are passed by value. The work done in the `stateBreak` function is discussed later.

If the state names are the same, the `stateBreak` function is not called. Instead the program continues with a test (line 46) to see if the city names are the same; it does this by using an `if` statement to test the second control break variable, `city`. This is done to determine if the record currently being processed has the same city as the previous record. If it does not, the beginning of a new city has been encountered, resulting in a call to the `cityBreak` function (line 47), which is one of the control break functions. Notice that three arguments—`total`, `prev`, and `city`—are passed to this function. The work done in the `cityBreak` function is discussed later.

If the names of the current city and state and the previous city and state are the same, neither of the control break functions is called. Instead, the program continues to:

» Add 1 to the total sales for the current city (line 48)

» Get the next input record (lines 49 through 62)

» Test the condition in the `while` loop again (line 42), thereby causing the loop to continue executing until the user enters the word "`done`" instead of a book's title

When the `while` loop is exited, the last section of this program executes. This consists of calling the `stateBreak` function again on line 65 to process totals for the previous record and then printing six tab characters, the value of the local constant named `FOOTER` along with the grand total of sales in all cities and states (`total[GRAND]`) on line 66.

Now, let's look at the two control break functions, `stateBreak` and `cityBreak`.

The `stateBreak` function does the following:

1. Declares the local constants `GRAND`, `STATE`, `CITY`, and `EXPLANATION` (lines 84 through 87).

2. Calls the `cityBreak` function on line 89, passing `total`, `prev`, and `city` to the function. This function is called because if the state has changed, the city has also changed. The beginning memory address of the arrays named `total` and `prev` are passed by value as discussed previously, and the `string` named `city`, is passed by value. The `cityBreak` function does the following:

    a. Declares local constants `GRAND`, `STATE`, and `CITY` (lines 72 through 74).

    b. Prints six tab characters, the name of the previous city (`prev[CITY]`) and that city's total sales (`total[CITY]`) (line 76).

    c. Adds the city's total sales to the total for the state (`total[STATE] += total[CITY];`) (line 77).

    d. Sets the value of `total[CITY]` to 0 to get ready for the next city (line 78).

    e. Assigns the current `city` to `prev[CITY]` to get ready for the next city (line 79).

    f. Passes control back to where this method was called (line 80).

3. Prints six tab characters, the value of the constant named EXPLANATION, the name of the previous state (prev[STATE]), and that state's total sales (total[STATE]) (line 90).

4. Adds the state's total sales to the grand total (total[GRAND] += total[STATE];) (line 91).

5. Sets the value of total[STATE] to 0 to get ready for the next state (line 92).

6. Assigns the current state to prev[STATE] to get ready for the next state (line 93).

7. Passes control back to the main function (line 94).

EXERCISE 8-2: MULTIPLE-LEVEL CONTROL BREAK PROGRAMS

In this exercise, you use what you have learned about multiple-level control break programs to answer specific questions. First, study the C++ code that follows:

```
if(floorNum != oldfloorNum)
    floorBreak();
else if (aisleNum != oldAisleNum)
    aisleBreak();
else if (rowNum != oldRowNum)
    rowBreak();
```

1. In this program, rowNum is used to determine when a major-level break should occur. True or false?

_____

2. How many control break variables does this program include?

_____

Name them.

_____

3. For this control break program, input records should be sorted by row within aisle within floor. True or false?

_____

LAB 8-2: MULTIPLE-LEVEL CONTROL BREAK PROGRAMS

In this lab, you use what you have learned about multiple-level control break programs to complete a C++ program. The program should produce a report for a used car dealer that includes the make and model of each car sold, the total cars sold of each make, and a total of all cars sold. The student file for this lab includes the variable declarations and input statements. You need to implement the control break portion of the program, which executes when a new record is read, that has a different make and/or a different model. Be sure to accumulate the car make totals and the grand total for all cars. Comments in the student file tell you where to write your code. You can use the Bookstore2 program in this chapter as a guide.

1. Open the source code file named `UsedCars.cpp` using Notepad or the text editor of your choice.

2. Study the prewritten code to understand what has already been done.

3. Write the control break code in the `main` function.

4. Write the `makeBreak` control break function.

5. Write the `modelBreak` control break function.

6. Save this source code file in a directory of your choice and then make that directory your working directory.

7. Compile the source code file `UsedCars.cpp`.

8. Execute the program.

Use the following input data.

Make	Model	Price	Color
Chevrolet	Corvette	52000	Silver
Chevrolet	Corvette	58000	Red
Chevrolet	Aveo	11000	Black
Ford	Mustang	23000	Blue
Ford	Focus	15000	Blue
Honda	Accord	28000	Red
Honda	Odyssey	36000	Silver
Honda	Civic	19000	Black

Your output should show that the total for Chevrolet Corvette is 2, the total for Chevrolet Aveo is 1, the total for Chevrolet is 3, the total for Ford Mustang is 1, the total for Ford Focus is 1, the total for Ford is 2, the total for Honda Accord is 1, the total for Honda Odyssey is 1, the total for Honda Civic is 1, and the total for Honda is 3. The grand total of cars sold is 8.

9

SORTING DATA AND FILE INPUT/OUTPUT

After studying this chapter, you will be able to:

Explain the need to sort data
Swap data values in a program
Create a bubble sort in C++
Explain and perform file handling

In the first three sections of this chapter, you review why you would want to sort data, how to use C++ to swap two data values in a program, and how to create a bubble sort in a C++ program. You should do the exercises and labs in this chapter after you have finished Chapter 9 in *Programming Logic and Design, Fifth Edition, Comprehensive*.

SORTING DATA

Data records are always stored in some order, but possibly not in the order in which you want to process or view them in your program. When this is the case, you need to give your program the ability to arrange (sort) records in a useful order. For example, the inventory records you need to process might be stored in product-number order, but you might need to produce a report that lists products from lowest cost to highest cost. That means your program needs to sort the records by cost.

Sorting makes searching for records easier and more efficient. Data can be sorted in **ascending order** (lowest to highest for numeric data, or alphabetically for text) or in **descending order** (highest to lowest for numeric data, or reverse alphabetical order for text). People can usually find what they are searching for by simply glancing through a group of data items; but a program must look through a group of data items one by one, making a decision about each one. When searching unsorted records for a particular data value, a program must examine every single record until it either locates the data value or determines that it does not exist. However, when searching sorted records, a program can quickly determine when to stop searching, as shown in the following step-by-step scenario:

1. The records used by your program are sorted in ascending order by product number.
2. The user is searching for the product number 12367.
3. The program locates the record for product number 12368 but has not yet found product number 12367.
4. The program determines that the record for product number 12367 does not exist, and therefore stops searching through the list.

Many search algorithms require that data be sorted before it can be searched. (An **algorithm** is a plan for solving a problem.) You can choose from many algorithms for sorting and searching for data. In *Programming Logic and Design, Fifth Edition, Comprehensive*, you learned about three sort algorithms: bubble sort, insertion sort, and selection sort. You also learned about a type of search algorithm: the binary search. Only the bubble sort algorithm is covered in this book.

SWAPPING DATA VALUES

Sorting involves swapping data values. When you swap values, you place the value stored in one variable into a second variable, and then you place the value in the second variable in the first variable. You must also create a third variable to temporarily hold one of the values you want to swap so that a value is not lost. For example, if you try to swap values using the following code, you will lose the value of `score2`:

```
int score1 = 90;
int score2 = 85;
score2 = score1;    // The value of score2 is now 90
score1 = score2;    // The value of score1 is also 90
```

However, if you use a variable to temporarily hold one of the values, the swap is successful. This is shown in the following code:

```
int score1 = 90;
int score2 = 85;
int temp;
temp = score2;      // The value of temp is 85
score2 = score1;    // The value of score2 is 90
score1 = temp;      // The value of score1 is 85
```

EXERCISE 9-1: SWAPPING VALUES

In this exercise, you use what you have learned about swapping values to complete the following:

1. Suppose you have declared and initialized two `string` variables, `item1` and `item2`, in a C++ program. Now, you want to swap the values stored in `item1` and `item2`, but only if the value of `item1` is greater than the value of `item2`. Write the C++ code that accomplishes this task. The declarations are as follows:

```
string item1 = "shirt";
string item2 = "shoes";
```

_____

_____

_____

_____

LAB 9-1: SWAPPING VALUES

In this lab, you complete a C++ program that swaps values stored in three `int` variables and determines maximum and minimum values. The C++ file provided for this lab contains the necessary variable declarations, as well as the input and output statements. You want to end up with the smallest value stored in the variable named `num1` and the largest value stored in the variable named `num3`. You need to write the statements that compare the values and swap them if appropriate. Comments included in the code tell you where to write your statements.

1. Open the source code file named `Swap.cpp` using the text editor of your choice.

2. Write the statements that test the first two integers, and swap them if necessary.

3. Write the statements that test the second and third integer and swap them if necessary.

4. Write the statements that test the first and second integers again and swap them if necessary.

5. Save this source code file in a directory of your choice and then make that directory your working directory.

6. Compile the source code file Swap.cpp.

7. Execute the program using the following sets of input values and record the output:

```
55 33 -1
60 99 37
32 54 32
```

USING A BUBBLE SORT

A bubble sort is one of the easiest sorting techniques to understand. However, while it is logically simple, it is not very efficient. If the list contains *n* values, the bubble sort will make *n - 1* passes over the list. For example, if the list contains 100 values, the bubble sort will make 99 passes over the data. During each pass, it examines successive overlapped pairs and swaps or exchanges those values that are out of order. After one pass over the data, the heaviest (largest) value has sunk to the bottom and is in the correct position in the list.

In *Programming Logic and Design, Fifth Edition*, you learned several ways to refine the bubble sort algorithm. One way is to reduce unnecessary comparisons by ignoring the last value in the list in the second pass through the data because you can be sure the last value is already positioned correctly. On the third pass, you can ignore the last two values in the list because you know they are already positioned correctly. Thus, in each pass, you can reduce the number of items to be compared, and possibly swapped, by one.

Another refinement to the bubble sort is to eliminate unnecessary passes over the data in the list. When items in the array to be sorted are not entirely out of order, it may not be necessary to make *n - 1* passes over the data because after several passes, they may already be in order. You can add a flag variable to the bubble sort program, and then test the value of that flag variable to determine whether any swaps have been made in any single pass over the data. If no swaps have been made, you know that the list is in order, and therefore you do not need to continue with additional passes.

In *Programming Logic and Design, Fifth Edition* and in this book, you have learned about using a constant for the size of the array to make your logic easier to understand and your programs easier to change and maintain. Finally, you have learned how to sort a list of varying size by counting the number of items placed in the array as you read items.

All of these refinements are included in the pseudocode for the score sorting program in Figure 9-1. The C++ code that implements the score sorting logic is provided in Figure 9-2. The line numbers shown in Figure 9-2 are not part of the C++ code. They are provided for reference only.

```
start
   num SIZE = 100
   num score[SIZE]
   num numberOfEls
   numberOfEls = fillArray(score, SIZE)
   sortArray(score, numberOfEls)
   displayArray(score, numberOfEls)
stop

num fillArray(num score[], num SIZE)
   num x = 0
   num limit = SIZE - 1
   get score[x]
   while not eof AND x < limit
      x = x + 1
      get score[x]
   endwhile
return x

void sortArray(num score[], num els)
   num x = 0
   num pairsToCompare = els - 1
   string switchOccurred = "Yes"
   while switchOccurred = "Yes"
      x = 0
      switchOccurred = "No"
      while x < pairsToCompare
         if score[x] > score[x + 1] then
            swap(score, x)
            switchOccurred = "Yes"
         endif
         x = x + 1
      endwhile
      pairsToCompare = pairsToCompare - 1
   endwhile
return

void swap(num score[], num x)
   num temp
   temp = score[x + 1]
   score[x + 1] = score[x]
   score[x] = temp
return

void displayArray(num score[], num els)
   num x = 0
   while x < els
      print score[x]
      x = x + 1
   endwhile
return
```

Figure 9-1 Pseudocode for score sorting program

```
1     // StudentScores.cpp - This program interactively reads a variable number
2     // of student test scores, stores the scores in an array, and then sorts the
3     // scores in ascending order.
4     // Input:   Interactive
5     // Output:  Sorted list of student scores
6
7     #include <iostream>
8     using namespace std;
9     int fillArray(int [], int);
10    void sortArray(int [], int);
11    void swap(int [], int);
12    void displayArray(int [], int);
13
14    int main()
15    {
16       // Declare variables
17       const int SIZE = 100;    // Maximum size of array
18       int score[SIZE];         // Array of student scores
19       int numberOfEls;         // Actual number of elements in array
20
21       numberOfEls = fillArray(score, SIZE);
22       sortArray(score, numberOfEls);
23       displayArray(score, numberOfEls);
24
25       return 0;
26    } // End of main function
27
28    int fillArray(int score[], int size)
29    {
30       int x = 0;
31       const int LIMIT = size - 1;
32       int stuScore = 0;
33       bool notDone = true;
34
35       cout << "Enter a student's score or 999 to quit: ";
36       cin >> stuScore;
37
38       // Test to see if user entered 999
39       if(stuScore == 999)
40          notDone = false;
41
42       while(notDone && x < LIMIT)
43       {
44          // Place value in array.
45          score[x] = stuScore;
46          x++;    // Get ready for next input item
47          cout << "Enter a student's score or done to quit: ";
48          cin >> stuScore;
49          // Test to see if user entered 999
50          if(stuScore == 999)
51             notDone = false;
52       }  // End of input loop
```

Figure 9-2 C++ code for score sorting program ▶

```
53
54        return x;
55    } // End of fillArray function
56
57    void sortArray(int score[], int els)
58    {
59        int x = 0;
60        int pairsToCompare = els - 1; // Number of items to compare
61        bool switchOccurred = true;          // Set flag to true.
62
63        // Outer loop controls number of passes over data
64        while(switchOccurred == true) // Test flag
65        {
66            x = 0;
67            switchOccurred = false;
68            // Inner loop controls number of items to compare
69            while(x < pairsToCompare)
70            {
71                if(score[x] > score[x+1]) // Swap?
72                {
73                    swap(score, x);
74                    switchOccurred = true;
75                }
76                x++;    // Get ready for next pair
77            }
78            pairsToCompare--;
79        }
80    } // End of sortArray function
81
82    void swap(int score[], int x)
83    {
84        int temp;
85        temp = score[x + 1];
86        score[x+1] = score[x];
87        score[x] = temp;
88    } // End of swap function
89
90    void displayArray(int score[], int els)
91    {
92        int x = 0;
93        while(x < els)
94        {
95            cout << score[x] << endl;
96            x++;
97        }
98    } // End of displayArray function
```

Figure 9-2 C++ code for score sorting program (*continued*)

THE main FUNCTION

As shown in Figure 9-2, the main function (line 14) declares variables and calls other functions that are responsible for performing the work of the program. The variables include: a constant named SIZE (line 17), initialized with the value 100, which represents the maximum number of items this program can sort; an array of data type int named score (line 18) that is used to store up to a maximum of SIZE items to be sorted; and an int named numberOfEls (line 19) that is used to hold the actual number of items stored in the array, which might be fewer than SIZE.

After these variables are declared, a function named fillArray is called on line 21. The fillArray function is responsible for filling the array with items to be sorted. The first argument, the score array, is passed to the function so that items can be placed in the array.

The second argument, SIZE, is passed by value to the fillArray function defining the maximum number of items that can be stored in the score array. (You learned about passing arguments by reference, by address, and by value in Chapter 7 of this book.) Notice that the call to the fillArray function is on the right side of an assignment operator. Also, the value returned by this function is assigned to the int variable named numberOfEls, which will contain the actual number of items placed in the array when this function returns.

Next, on line 22, the sortArray function is called with score (the array of ints) and numberOfEls (the actual number of items in the array that need to be sorted). This function is responsible for sorting the items stored in the score array. Lastly, the displayArray function is called on line 23 with the score array and numberOfEls passed to it. This function is responsible for displaying the sorted scores on the user's screen.

THE fillArray FUNCTION

The fillArray function, which begins on line 28 in Figure 9-2, receives two arguments: int score[] and int size. This function is responsible for: 1) storing the data in the array; and 2) counting the actual number of elements placed in the array. The fillArray function returns the number of elements to the main function.

Within the fillArray function, variables and constants are declared and initialized where appropriate (lines 30 through 33). Next, on lines 35 and 36, a priming read retrieves the first student score from the user. Notice that, as in the programs in Chapter 8 of this book, the C++ code in the priming read is different than the pseudocode. The cout statement that asks users to input a student's score also instructs them to enter 999 (a sentinel value) when they are finished inputting scores. Also, an if statement is used on line 39 to test whether the user entered a student's score or the value 999. If the user is done entering scores, the result of this test will be true, causing the bool value false to be assigned to the variable named notDone on line 40. The bool variable named notDone is used later in the program to control the while loop.

Next, on line 42, the condition that controls the while loop is tested. The while loop executes as long as the value of the bool variable notDone is true and the number of scores input by the user (represented by the variable named x) is less than LIMIT. If x is less than LIMIT, there is enough room in the array to store the student score. In that case, the program assigns the student score, stuScore, to the array named score using the value of x as a subscript to specify the position in the array (line 45). The program then increments the value of x on line 46 to get ready to store the next student score in the array. Lines 47 through 51 are responsible for getting the next student's score and testing it using the same technique used in the priming read. The loop continues to execute until the user enters the value 999 or until there is no more room in the array.

When the program exits the loop, the return statement on line 54 returns the value of x to the main function. Notice that the array subscript variable x is initialized to 0 because the first position in an array is position 0. Also, notice that the value of x is incremented every time the while loop executes; therefore, x represents the number of student scores the user entered.

THE sortArray FUNCTION

In the sortArray function, the program uses a refined bubble sort to rearrange the student scores in the array named score in ascending order. Refer to Figure 9-1, which includes the pseudocode, and Figure 9-2, which includes the C++ code that implements the sortArray function.

As you can see on line 57 in Figure 9-2, this function receives two arguments: int score[] (the array of items to sort) and int els (the number of scores stored in the array). Lines 59 through 61 declare variables. Notice on line 60 that the variable pairsToCompare is initialized with a value that represents the number of pairs that will be compared in the first pass of the bubble sort. The number of pairs is calculated by subtracting 1 from els, the number of elements in the array. This ensures that the program does not attempt to compare item x with item x+1, when x is the last item in the array. Line 61 initializes the flag variable, switchOccurred, to true because, at this point in the program, it is assumed that items will need to be swapped.

The outer loop, while(switchOccurred == true), controls the number of passes over the data. This logic implements one of the refinements discussed earlier—eliminating unnecessary passes over the data. As long as switchOccurred is true, the program knows that swaps have been made and that, therefore, the data is still out of order. Thus, when switchOccurred is true, the program enters the loop. The first statement in the body of the loop (line 66) is x = 0;. The program assigns the value 0 to x because x is used as the array subscript. Recall, in C++, the first subscript in an array is 0.

Next, to prepare for comparing the elements in the array, line 67 assigns the value false to switchOccurred. This is necessary because the program has not yet swapped any values in the array on this pass. The inner loop begins on line 69. The test x < pairsToCompare controls the number of pairs of values in the array that the program compares on one pass over the data. This implements another of the refinements discussed earlier—reducing unnecessary comparisons. The last statement in the outer loop (line 78), pairsToCompare--;, decrements the value of pairsToCompare by 1 each time the outer loop executes. The program decrements pairsToCompare because when a complete pass is made over the data, it knows an item is positioned in the array correctly. Comparing the value of pairsToCompare with the value of x in the inner loop reduces the number of necessary comparisons made when this loop executes.

On line 71, within the inner loop, adjacent items in the array are accessed and compared using the subscript variable x and x+1. The adjacent array items are compared to see if the program should swap them. If the values should be swapped, the program calls the swap function on line 73, which uses the technique discussed earlier to rearrange the two values in the array. Next, line 74 assigns true to the variable named switchOccurred. The last task performed by the inner loop (line 76) is to add 1 to the value of the subscript variable x. This ensures that the next time through the inner loop, the program compares the next two adjacent items in the array. The program continues to compare two adjacent items and possibly swap them as long as the value of x is less than the value of pairsToCompare.

THE displayArray FUNCTION

In the displayArray function, the program prints the sorted array on the user's screen. Figure 9-1 shows the pseudocode for this function. The C++ code is shown in Figure 9-2.

In line 90 of Figure 9-2, the following are passed to the displayArray function: the array named score[] (which is now sorted) and the int variable named els, which contains the number of sorted items in the array. Next, line 92 assigns the value 0 to the subscript variable x. This is done before the while loop is entered because the first item stored in the array is referenced using the subscript value 0. The loop in lines 93 through 97 prints all of the values in the array named score by incrementing the value of the subscript variable x each time the loop executes. The displayArray function then returns control (line 98) to the main function, where the statement return 0; (line 25) executes and ends the program.

EXERCISE 9-2: USING A BUBBLE SORT

In this exercise, you use what you have learned about sorting data using a bubble sort. Study the following C++ code and then answer the questions that follow:

```cpp
int numbers[] = {6, 44, -2, 88, 242, 400, 30};
const int NUM_ITEMS = 7;
int j, k, temp;
int numPasses = 0, numCompares = 0, numSwaps = 0;
for(j = 0; j < NUM_ITEMS - 1; j++)
{
    numPasses++;
    for(k = 0; k < NUM_ITEMS - 1; k++)
    {
        numCompares++;
        if(numbers[k] > numbers[k+1])
        {
            numSwaps++;
            temp = numbers[k+1];
            numbers[k+1] = numbers[k];
            numbers[k] = temp;
        }
    }
}
```

1. Does this code perform an ascending sort or a descending sort? How do you know?

   _____

2. Exactly how many passes are made over the data in the array? Specify a number.

   _____

3. How many comparisons are made? Specify a number.

   _____

4. Do the variables named `numPasses`, `numCompares`, and `numSwaps` accurately keep track of the number of passes, compares, and swaps made in this bubble sort? Explain your answer.

   _____

LAB 9-2: USING A BUBBLE SORT

In this lab, you complete a C++ program that uses an array to store data for a computer programming teacher. The program is similar to the program described in Chapter 9, Exercise 3 in *Programming Logic and Design, Fifth Edition*. The program should allow the user to enter a student's name and 10 quiz scores. The program should output the student's name and his or her eight highest quiz scores. The file provided for this lab contains the necessary variable declarations and input statements. You need to write the code that sorts the scores in ascending order using a bubble sort, and then print the student's name and eight highest quiz scores. Comments in the code tell you where to write your statements.

1. Open the source code file named `QuizScores.cpp` using Notepad or the text editor of your choice.

2. Write the bubble sort and the swap function.

3. Output the student's name and eight highest quiz scores.

4. Save this source code file in a directory of your choice and then make that directory your working directory.

5. Compile the source code file `QuizScores.cpp`.

6. Execute the program with the following input and record the output:

   Student Name: `William Moriarty`

   Ten Quiz Scores: `85, 42, 76, 95, 90, 85, 82, 92, 96, 88`

FILE INPUT AND OUTPUT

You should do the exercises and labs in this section after you have finished Chapter 10 in *Programming Logic and Design, Fifth Edition, Comprehensive*.

Business applications typically have to manipulate large amounts of data. This data is stored in one or more files. As you learned in Chapter 1 of *Programming Logic and Design, Fifth Edition*, data is organized in a hierarchy. At the lowest level of the hierarchy is a **field**, which is a group of characters. On the next level up is a **record**, which is a group of related fields. For example, you could write a program that processes employee records where each employee record consists of three fields: the employee's first name, the employee's last name, and the employee's department number.

In C++, to use the data stored in a file, the program must first open the file and then read the data from the file. You use prewritten classes that are part of a C++ library to accomplish this. Next, you learn how to use these classes to open a file, close a file, read data from a file, and write data to a file.

USING INPUT AND OUTPUT CLASSES

To use the classes that you need to perform file input (`ifstream`) and output (`ofstream`), you must add the following preprocessor directive at the beginning of your C++ program:

```
#include <fstream>
```

The classes included in the `fstream` class are prewritten for you by the C++ development team and allow you to simplify your programming tasks by creating objects using these classes. You can then use the attributes and methods of these objects in your C++ programs.

OPENING A FILE FOR READING

> **▶▶NOTE**
> You can think of `ifstream` as the data type for input files. In the next chapter, you will learn that `ifstream` is actually a class and `data_in` is an object.

To open a file in C++ to read data into your program, you declare a file input stream object (variable) as shown below:

```
ifstream data_in;
```

You then use the `open` method (function) to specify the name of the file to open. Look at the following example:

```
data_in.open("inputFile.dat");
```

In the example, you use the `ifstream` object (`data_in`), followed by a dot (`.`), followed by the name of the method (`open`) to open a file for input. Within the parentheses, you place the name of the file you want to open enclosed in double quotes. This statement opens the file named `inputFile.dat` for reading. This means that the program can now read data from the file. In this example, the file named `inputFile.dat` must be saved in the same folder as the C++ program that is using the file. To open a file that is saved in a different folder, a path must be specified as in the next example:

```
data_in.open("C:\myC++Programs\Chapter9\inputFile.dat");
```

READING DATA FROM AN INPUT FILE

Once you have opened the input file, you are ready to read the data in the file. You can use the extraction operator >> just as you used it with `cin`.

In the next example, we will assume that the input file for a program is organized so that an employee's first name is on one line, followed by the employee's last name on the next line, followed by his or her salary on the third, as follows:

Tim
Moriarty
2000.00

To allow the program to read this data, you would write the following C++ code:

```
ifstream data_in;
string firstName, lastName;
double salary;
data_in.open("inputFile.dat");
data_in >> firstName;
data_in >> lastName;
data_in >> salary;
```

The first line in the example declares `data_in`, an `ifstream` object. The second line declares two `string` variables named `firstName` and `lastName`. The third line declares a `double` named `salary`. Next, `data_in` is used with the `open` method to open the file named `inputFile.dat`. The extraction operator (`>>`) is then used three times to read the three lines of input from the file (`inputFile.dat`) associated with `data_in`. After this code executes, the variable named `firstName` contains the value Tim, the variable named `lastName` contains the value Moriarty, and the variable named `salary` contains the value 2000.00.

READING DATA USING A LOOP AND EOF

In a program that has to read large amounts of data, it is usually best to use a loop. In the loop, the program continues to read from the file until EOF (end of file) is encountered. In C++, the `eof` method (function) returns a `true` value when EOF is reached and a `false` value when EOF has not been reached. The `eof` method can be used with `cin` for keyboard input or with an `ifstream` object, such as `data_in`.

The C++ code that follows shows how to use the `eof` method as part of a loop:

```
ifstream data_in;
string firstName;
data_in.open("inputFile.dat");
data_in >> firstName;
while(!(data_in.eof()))
{
    cout << firstName;
    data_in >> firstName;
}
```

> **» NOTE**
> For keyboard input, you enter the EOF character by typing Ctrl + Z (Windows) or Ctrl + D (UNIX/Linux).

In this example, a priming read is used on the fourth line, `data_in >> firstName;`, and then the `eof` method is used as the expression to be tested in the `while` loop. As long as the value returned by `eof` is not equal to `true`, the expression is `true` and the loop is entered.

Notice the negation operator (!) is used to reverse the value returned by the eof method. As soon as EOF is encountered, the test becomes false and the program exits the loop. The parentheses that surround the eof method call are used to control precedence.

OPENING A FILE FOR WRITING

To write data from a C++ program to an output file, the program must first open a file. Similar to input files, you must first declare a file stream object (variable). For output files, you declare an output stream object as shown below:

```
ofstream data_out;
```

You then use the open method (function) to specify the name of the file to open. Look at the following example:

```
data_out.open("outputFile.dat");
```

In the example, you use the ofstream object (data_out), followed by a dot (.), followed by the name of the method (open) to open a file for output. Within the parentheses, you place the name of the file you want to open enclosed in double quotes. This statement opens the file named outputFile.dat for writing. This means that the program can now write data to the file. In this example, the file named outputFile.dat is saved in the same folder as the C++ program that is using the file. To open a file that is saved in a different folder, a path must be specified as in the next example:

```
data_out.open("C:\myC++Programs\Chapter9\outputFile.dat");
```

WRITING DATA TO AN OUTPUT FILE

Once you have opened the output file, you are ready to write data to the file. You can use the insertion operator << just as you used it with cout.

As an example, assume that an employee's firstName, lastName, and salary have been read from an input file as in the previous example, and that the employee is to receive a 15% salary increase that is calculated as follows:

```
const double INCREASE = 1.15;
double newSalary;
newSalary = salary * INCREASE;
```

You now want to write the employee's firstName, lastName, and newSalary to the output file named outputFile.dat. The code that follows accomplishes this task:

```
ofstream data_out;
data_out.open("outputFile.dat");
data_out << firstName << endl;
data_out << lastName << endl;
data_out << newSalary << endl;
data_out.close();
```

The last line in the previous example uses data_out and the close method to close the output file. It is a good programming practice to close input and output files when they are no longer needed by a program. The C++ program `fileIOTest.cpp` shown in Figure 9-3 implements the file input and output operations discussed in this section.

```cpp
// fileIOTest.cpp
// Input:  inputFile.dat
// Output: outputFile.dat

#include <fstream>
#include <iostream>
#include <string>
using namespace std;
int main()
{
    string firstName;
    string lastName;
    double salary;
    double new_salary;
    const double INCREASE = 1.15;
    ifstream data_in;
    ofstream data_out;

    // Open input and output file
    data_in.open("inputFile.dat");
    data_out.open("outputFile.dat");

    // Read record from input file
    data_in >> firstName;
    data_in >> lastName;
    data_in >> salary;
    // Calculate new salary
    new_salary = salary * INCREASE;
    // Write record to output file
    data_out << firstName << endl;
    data_out << lastName << endl;
    data_out << new_salary << endl;
    // Close files
    data_in.close();
    data_out.close();
    return 0;
} // End of main function
```

Figure 9-3 Reading and writing file data

When writing code that opens files and writes to files, you need to be aware of two potential problems: first, the program might try to open a nonexistent file; and second, it might try to read beyond the EOF marker. You will learn how to handle these error situations as you learn more about C++. They are beyond the scope of this book.

EXERCISE 9-3: OPENING FILES AND PERFORMING FILE INPUT

In this exercise, you use what you have learned about opening a file and getting input into a program from a file to answer some questions about the code shown in Figure 9-4.

```
1      ofstream data_in;
2      data_in.open(myVideoFile.dat);
3      string videoName, videoPrice, videoShelf;
4      data_in >> videoShelf;
5      data_in >> videoPrice;
6      data_in >> videoName;
```

Figure 9-4 Code for Exercise 9-3

1. Describe the error on line 1 and explain how to fix it.

   _____

2. Describe the error on line 2 and explain how to fix it.

   _____

3. Consider the following data from the input file myVideoFile.dat:

   Shrek 13.00 1A

   Jaws 14.00 2C

   Casablanca 17.00 3B

   a. What value is stored in the variable named videoName?

   _____

   b. What value is stored in the variable named videoPrice?

   _____

   c. What value is stored in the variable named videoShelf?

   _____

   d. If there is a problem with the values of these variables, what is the problem and how could you fix it?

   _____

LAB 9-3: USING AN INPUT FILE

In this lab, you open a file and read input from that file in a prewritten C++ program. The program should read and print the names of fish that are stored in the input file named fish.dat.

1. Open the source code file named `Fish.cpp` using Notepad or the text editor of your choice.

2. Declare the variables you will need.

3. Write the C++ statements that will open the input file `fish.dat` for reading.

4. Include statements to print a heading and perform a priming read. Then, write a `while` loop to read the input until EOF is reached.

5. In the body of the loop, print the name of each fish and read the next fish. When the loop is exited, remember to close the file.

6. Save this source code file in a directory of your choice and then make that directory your working directory.

7. Compile the source code file `Fish.cpp`.

8. Execute the program.

10

OBJECT-ORIENTED C++

After studying this chapter, you will be able to:

Explain introductory object-oriented concepts
Create a simple programmer-defined class
Use a programmer-defined class in a C++ program
Use inheritance to create a derived C++ class
Use a derived class in a C++ program

Note that this chapter covers topics that include the material covered in Chapter 11 in *Programming Logic and Design, Fifth Edition, Comprehensive* by Joyce Farrell.

A PROGRAMMER-DEFINED CLASS

Before you continue with this chapter, you should take a moment to review the object-oriented terminology (`class`, `attribute`, and `method`) presented in Chapter 1 of this book and in Chapter 11 of *Programming Logic and Design, Fifth Edition, Comprehensive*.

You have been using prewritten classes, objects, and methods throughout this book. For example, you have used the `open` method that is a member of the `ifstream` and `ofstream` class to open input and output files. In this section, you learn how to create your own class that includes attributes and methods of your choice. In programming terminology, a class created by the programmer is referred to as a **programmer-defined class** or a **custom class**.

To review, remember that procedural programming focuses on: 1) declaring data; 2) defining functions that are separate from the data; and 3) calling those functions to operate on the data. This is the style of programming you have been using in Chapters 1 through 9 of this book. Object-oriented programming also focuses on data and the functions that you need to manipulate that data. However, object-oriented programming is quite different from procedural programming. Data and functions (which are called "methods" in object-oriented programming) are **encapsulated**, or contained, within a class. Individual objects are created as an instance of a class. The program tells an object to perform tasks by passing messages to it. Such a message consists of an instruction to execute one of the class's methods. The class method then manipulates the data (which is part of the object itself).

CREATING A PROGRAMMER-DEFINED CLASS

In Chapter 11 of *Programming Logic and Design, Fifth Edition, Comprehensive*, you studied pseudocode for the `Employee` class. This pseudocode is shown in Figure 10-1. The C++ code that implements the `Employee` class is shown in Figure 10-2.

```
1     class Employee
2         string lastName
3         num hourlyWage
4         num weeklyPay
5
6         void setLastName(string name)
7             lastName = name
8         return
9
10        void setHourlyWage(num wage)
11            hourlyWage = wage
12            calculateWeeklyPay()
13        return
```

Figure 10-1 Pseudocode for Employee class ▶

```
14
15        string getLastName()
16        return lastName
17
18        num getHourlyWage()
19        return hourlyWage
20
21        num getWeeklyPay()
22        return weeklyPay
23
24        void calculateWeeklyPay()
25           num WORK_WEEK_HOURS = 40
26           weeklyPay = hourlyWage * WORK_WEEK_HOURS
27        return
28     endClass
```

Figure 10-1 Pseudocode for Employee class (*continued*)

```
1      // Employee.cpp
2      #include <string>
3      using namespace std;
4      class Employee
5      {
6         public:
7            void setLastName(string);
8            void setHourlyWage(double);
9            double getHourlyWage();
10           double getWeeklyPay();
11           string getLastName();
12        private:
13           string lastName;
14           double hourlyWage;
15           double weeklyPay;
16           void calculateWeeklyPay();
17     }; // You end a class definition with a semicolon
18
19     void Employee::setLastName(string name)
20     {
21        lastName = name;
22        return;
23     }
24     void Employee::setHourlyWage(double wage)
25     {
26        hourlyWage = wage;
27        calculateWeeklyPay();
28        return;
29     }
```

Figure 10-2 Employee class implemented in C++   ▶

179

```
30    string Employee::getLastName()
31    {
32        return lastName;
33    }
34    double Employee::getHourlyWage()
35    {
36        return hourlyWage;
37    }
38    double Employee::getWeeklyPay()
39    {
40        return weeklyPay;
41    }
42    void Employee::calculateWeeklyPay()
43    {
44        const int WORK_WEEK_HOURS = 40;
45        weeklyPay = hourlyWage * WORK_WEEK_HOURS;
46        return;
47    }
```

Figure 10-2 Employee class implemented in C++ (*continued*)

Looking at line 1 of the pseudocode in Figure 10-1, you see that you begin creating a class by specifying that it is a class. Looking at the C++ code in Figure 10-2, you see that line 1 is a comment, line 2 is a preprocessor directive, #include <string>, and line 3 is a using statement, using namespace std;. (You learned about preprocessor directives and using statements in Chapter 1 of this book.) This is followed by the class declaration for the Employee class on line 4. It begins with the keyword class, which specifies that what follows is a C++ class. The opening curly brace on line 5 and the closing curly brace on line 17 mark the beginning and the end of the class.

Notice that the closing curly brace on line 17 is followed by a semicolon. This closing curly brace is *absolutely necessary* because it is part of the C++ syntax for creating a class. Omitting this semicolon is a common error.

ADDING ATTRIBUTES TO A CLASS

The next step is to define the attributes (data) that are included in the Employee class. As shown on lines 2, 3, and 4 of the pseudocode in Figure 10-1, there are three attributes in this pseudocode class: string lastName, num hourlyWage, and num weeklyPay.

Lines 13, 14, and 15 in Figure 10-2 include these attributes in the C++ version of the Employee class. Notice in the C++ code that hourlyWage and weeklyPay are defined using the double data type and lastName is defined as a string. Also, notice that all three attributes are included in the **private** section of the class. The private section is defined by including the keyword private followed by a colon on line 12. As explained in *Programming Logic and Design, Fifth Edition, Comprehensive*, this means the data cannot be accessed by any method (function) that is not part of the class. Programs that use the Employee class must use the methods that are part of the class to access private data.

ADDING METHODS TO A CLASS

The next step is to add methods to the Employee class. The pseudocode versions of these methods, shown on lines 6 through 27 in Figure 10-1, are nonstatic methods. As you learned in Chapter 11 of *Programming Logic and Design, Fifth Edition, Comprehensive*, **nonstatic** methods are methods that are meant to be used with an object created from a class. In other words, to use these methods, we must create an object of the Employee class first and then use that object to **invoke** (or call) the method.

The code shown in Figure 10-2 shows how to include methods in the Employee class using C++. We will start the discussion with the set methods. You learned in *Programming Logic and Design, Fifth Edition, Comprehensive* that **set methods** are those whose purpose is to set the values of attributes (data fields) within the class. There are three data fields in the Employee class but we will only add two set methods: setLastName and setHourlyWage. We will not add a setWeeklyPay method because the weeklyPay data field will be set by the setHourlyWage method. The setHourlyWage method uses another method, calculateWeeklyPay, to accomplish this.

The setLastName method is shown on lines 19 through 23 in Figure 10-2, and the setHourlyWage method is shown on lines 24 through 29. Also notice that these two methods are declared in the public section of the class on lines 7 and 8. The public section of the class is specified by using the keyword public followed by a colon on line 6. Including methods in the **public** section means that programs may use these methods to gain access to the private data. The calculateWeeklyPay method, shown on lines 42 through 47 in Figure 10-2, is private, which means it can only be called from within another method that already belongs to the class. Notice that the calculateWeeklyPay method is declared in the private section in the Employee class on line 16. The calculateWeeklyPay method is called from the setHourlyWage method (line 27), and ensures that the class retains full control over when and how the calculateWeeklyPay method is used.

The setLastName method (lines 19 through 23) begins with the keyword void, followed by the name of the class, Employee, followed by the scope resolution operator (::), followed by the name of the method, setLastName. The **scope resolution operator** is used to associate the method with the class. In this case, the setLastName method is associated with the Employee class. The setLastName method accepts one argument, string name, that is assigned to the private attribute lastName. This sets the value of lastName. The setLastName method is a void method—that is, it returns nothing. Notice that the declaration of the setLastName method on line 7 agrees with the method definition; that is, both specify a return value of void and a single string argument.

The setHourlyWage method (lines 24 through 29) accepts one argument, double wage, that is assigned to the private attribute hourlyWage. This sets the value of hourlyWage. Next, it calls the private method calculateWeeklyPay on line 27. The calculateWeeklyPay method does not accept arguments. Within the method, on line 44, a constant, const int WORK_WEEK_HOURS, is declared and initialized with the value 40. The calculateWeeklyPay method then calculates weekly pay (line 45) by multiplying the private attribute hourlyWage by WORK_WEEK_HOURS. The result is assigned to the private attribute weeklyPay.

The `setHourlyWage` method and the `calculateWeeklyPay` method are `void` methods, which means they return nothing.

›› NOTE
It is not a requirement to use the prefix "get" when naming get methods; but by naming them using the word "get", their intended purpose is clearer.

The final step in creating the `Employee` class is adding the get methods. **Get methods** are methods that return a value to the program using the class. The pseudocode in Figure 10-1 includes three get methods: `getLastName` on lines 15 and 16, `getHourlyWage` on lines 18 and 19, and `getWeeklyPay` on lines 21 and 22. Lines 30 through 41 in Figure 10-2 illustrate the C++ version of the get methods in the `Employee` class.

In this class, the three get methods are `public` methods and accept no arguments. The `getLastName` method, shown on lines 30 through 33, returns a `string`, which is the value of the `private` attribute `lastName`. The `getHourlyWage` method, shown on lines 34 through 37, returns a `double`, which is the value of the `private` attribute `hourlyWage`; and the `getWeeklyPay` method, shown on lines 38 through 41, also returns a `double`, which is the value of the `private` attribute `weeklyPay`. The three get methods are declared in the `Employee` class on lines 9, 10, and 11.

The `Employee` class is now complete and may be used in a C++ program. The `Employee` class does not contain a `main` method (function) because it is not an application but rather a class that an application may now use to instantiate objects. The completed `Employee` class is included in the student files provided for this book, in a file named `Employee.cpp`.

Figure 10-3 illustrates a program named `MyEmployeeClassProgram` that uses the `Employee` class.

```
1    // This program uses the programmer-defined Employee class.
2    #include "Employee.cpp"
3    #include <iostream>
4    using namespace std;
5
6    int main()
7    {
8        const double LOW = 9.00;
9        const double HIGH = 14.65;
10       Employee myGardener;
11
12       myGardener.setLastName("Greene");
13       myGardener.setHourlyWage(LOW);
14       cout << "My gardener makes " << myGardener.getWeeklyPay()
             << " per week." << endl;
15
16       myGardener.setHourlyWage(HIGH);
17       cout << "My gardener makes " << myGardener.getWeeklyPay()
             << " per week." << endl;
18       return 0;
19   }
```

Figure 10-3 `MyEmployeeClassProgram` that uses the `Employee` class

As shown in Figure 10-3, the `MyEmployeeClassProgram` begins with a comment on line 1, followed by the preprocessor directive `#include "Employee.cpp"` on line 2. This preprocessor directive instructs the C++ compiler to include the file named `Employee.cpp`. The `Employee.cpp` file contains the `Employee` class declaration and the implementation of the methods defined in the `Employee` class. Notice that the file named `Employee.cpp` is enclosed in double quotes. The double quotes specify that this is a user-created file rather than a C++ header file. C++ header file names are surrounded by angle brackets as shown on line 3, which instructs the C++ compiler to include the C++ `iostream` header file. Line 4 includes a `using` statement that specifies the `std` namespace.

Since this is a C++ program, it must contain a `main` function. The `main` function begins on line 6. On lines 7 and 19, you see the opening and closing curly braces that define the beginning and end of the `main` function. Within the `main` function, two constants, LOW and HIGH, are declared and initialized on lines 8 and 9, respectively. Next, on line 10, an `Employee` object (an instance of the `Employee` class) is created with the following statement:

```
Employee myGardener;
```

In C++, a statement that creates a new object consists of the class name followed by the object's name. In the preceding example, the class is `Employee` and the name of the object is `myGardener`.

As you learned in *Programming Logic and Design, Fifth Edition, Comprehensive,* a **constructor** is a method that creates an object. You also learned that you can use a default constructor, which is a constructor that expects no arguments and is created automatically by the compiler for every class you write. The `Employee` constructor used in the `MyEmployeeClassProgram` is an example of a prewritten default constructor.

> **» NOTE**
> You can also write your own constructors if you wish. You will learn more about additional constructors in C++ courses you take after this course.

Once the `myGardener` object is created, you can use `myGardener` to invoke the set methods to set the value of `lastName` to `"Greene"` and the `hourlyWage` to LOW. The syntax used is shown in the following code sample:

```
myGardener.setLastName("Greene");
myGardener.setHourlyWage(LOW);
```

This is the syntax used to invoke a method with an instance (an object) of a class.

> **» NOTE** Notice the syntax `objectName.methodName`, in which the name of the object is separated from the name of the method by a dot.

On line 14 in Figure 10-3, the program then prints "`My gardener makes `" (a string constant) followed by the return value of `myGardener.getWeeklyPay()`, followed by the string constant "` per week.`", followed by a newline. Here, the `myGardener` object is used again—this time to invoke the `getWeeklyPay` method.

> **» NOTE**
> A dot is actually a period.

On line 16, `myGardener` invokes the set method `setHourlyWage` to specify a new value for `hourlyWage`. This time, `hourlyWage` is set to HIGH. The program then prints (line 17) "`My gardener makes `" (a string constant) followed by the return value of myGardener.getWeeklyPay, followed by the string constant " per week.", followed by a newline. The return 0; statement on line 18 ends the program. The output from this program is shown in Figure 10-4.

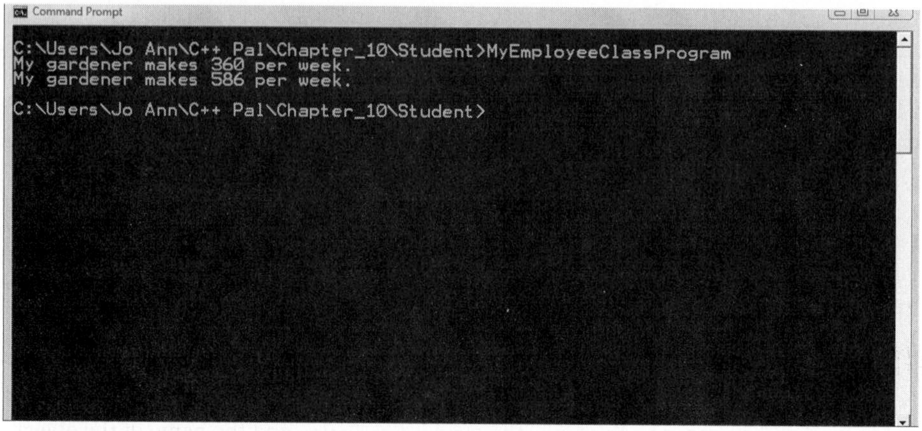

Figure 10-4 Output from MyEmployeeClassProgram

You will find the completed program in a file named MyEmployeeClassProgram.cpp included with the student files for this book.

EXERCISE 10-1: CREATING A CLASS IN C++

In this exercise, you use what you have learned about creating and using a programmer-defined class to answer some questions about the following code:

```cpp
class Circle
{
    public:
        void setRadius(double);
        double getRadius();
        double calculateCircumference();
        double calculateArea();
    private:
        double radius;    // Radius of this circle
        const double PI = 3.14159;
    };

void Circle::setRadius(double rad)
{
    radius = rad;
}
double Circle::getRadius()
{
    return radius;
}
```

```
double Circle::calculateCircumference()
{
    return (2 * PI * radius);
}
double Circle::calculateArea()
{
    return(PI * radius * radius);
}
```

In the following exercise, you should assume that a `Circle` object named `myCircle` has been created in a program that uses the `Circle` class, and `radius` is given a value as shown in the following code:

```
Circle myCircle;
myCircle.setRadius(3.0);
```

1. What is the output when the following line of C++ code executes?

   ```
   cout << "The circumference is : " <<
       myCircle.calculateCircumference();
   ```

   _____

2. Is the following a legal C++ statement? Why or why not?

   ```
   cout << "The area is : " << calculateArea();
   ```

   _____

3. Consider the following C++ code. What is the value stored in the `myCircle` object's attribute named `radius`?

   ```
   myCircle.setRadius(4.0);
   ```

   _____

4. Write the C++ code that will assign the circumference of `myCircle` to a `double` variable named `circumferenceOne`.

   _____

LAB 10-1: CREATING A CLASS IN C++

In this lab, you create a programmer-defined class and then use it in a C++ program. The program should create two `Rectangle` objects and find their area and perimeter. Use the `Circle` class that you worked with in Exercise 10-1 as a guide.

1. Open the class file named `Rectangle.cpp` using Notepad or the text editor of your choice.

2. In the `Rectangle` class, create two `private` attributes named `length` and `width`. Both `length` and `width` should be data type `double`.

3. Write `public` set methods to set the values for `length` and `width`.

4. Write `public` get methods to retrieve the values for `length` and `width`.

5. Write a `public calculateArea()` method and a `public calculatePerimeter()` method to calculate and return the area of the rectangle and the perimeter of the rectangle.

6. Save this class file, `Rectangle.cpp`, in a directory of your choice and then open the file named `MyRectangleClassProgram.cpp`.

7. In the `MyRectangleClassProgram`, create two `Rectangle` objects named `rectangleOne` and `rectangleTwo` using the default constructor as you saw in `MyEmployeeClassProgram.cpp`.

8. Set the `length` of `rectangleOne` to 4.0 and the `width` to 6.0. Set the `length` of `rectangleTwo` to 9.0 and the `width` to 7.0.

9. Print the value of `rectangleOne`'s perimeter and area, and then print the value of `rectangleTwo`'s perimeter and area.

10. Save `MyRectangleClassProgram.cpp` in the same directory as `Rectangle.cpp`.

11. Compile the source code file `MyRectangleClassProgram.cpp`.

12. Execute the program.

13. Record the output below.

_____

_____

_____

_____

REUSING C++ CLASSES

You can reuse classes and reuse the code that is written for the members of a class by taking advantage of inheritance. **Inheritance** allows you to create a new class that is based on an existing class. To use inheritance, you create a new class (called the **derived class**) that contains the members of the original class (called the **base class**). You can then modify the derived class by adding new members that allow it to behave in new ways. You can also redefine methods that are inherited from the base class if they do not meet your exact needs in the derived class.

For example, if you have an existing `Vehicle` class, you could derive a new class named `Automobile` from the `Vehicle` class. You could also derive a `TaxiCab` class, a `Motorcycle` class, or a `GoKart` class from the `Vehicle` class. In C++, any class can serve as a base class.

DEFINING A DERIVED CLASS
Let's begin by taking a look at the base class, `Vehicle`. Figure 10-5 contains the C++ code that implements the `Vehicle` class.

```
1       // Vehicle.cpp
2       #include <iostream>
3       using namespace std;
4       class Vehicle
5       {
6          public:
7              void setSpeed(double);
8              double getSpeed();
9              void accelerate(double);
10             void setFuelCapacity(double);
11             double getFuelCapacity();
12             void setMaxSpeed(double);
13             double getMaxSpeed();
14         private:
15             double fuelCapacity;
16             double maxSpeed;
17             double currentSpeed;
18      };
19
20      void Vehicle::setSpeed(double speed)
21      {
22         currentSpeed = speed;
23         return;
24      }
25
26      double Vehicle::getSpeed()
27      {
28         return currentSpeed;
29      }
30
31      void Vehicle::accelerate(double mph)
32      {
33         if(currentSpeed + mph < maxSpeed)
34             currentSpeed = currentSpeed + mph;
35         else
36             cout << "This vehicle cannot go that fast." << endl;
37      }
38
39      void Vehicle::setFuelCapacity(double fuel)
40      {
41         fuelCapacity = fuel;
42      }
43
44      double Vehicle::getFuelCapacity()
45      {
46         return fuelCapacity;
47      }
```

Figure 10-5 Vehicle class implemented in C++ ▶

```
48
49      void Vehicle::setMaxSpeed(double max)
50      {
51          maxSpeed = max;
52      }
53
54      double Vehicle::getMaxSpeed()
55      {
56          return maxSpeed;
57      }
```

Figure 10-5 Vehicle class implemented in C++ (*continued*)

The Vehicle class contains three private attributes: fuelCapacity, maxSpeed, and currentSpeed (lines 15 through 17). The Vehicle class also contains seven methods that are declared in the public section (lines 7 through 13). The methods are setSpeed, getSpeed, accelerate, setFuelCapacity, getFuelCapacity, setMaxSpeed, and getMaxSpeed. The methods are implemented on lines 20 through 57. Read over the C++ code written for these methods to be sure you understand them. Three of the methods are set methods and are written in a similar manner as the set methods that belong to the Employee class discussed in the previous section. Three of the methods are get methods and are written in a similar manner as the get methods that belong to the Employee class discussed in the previous section. Note that the accelerate method contains something you have not yet seen. The if statement that is part of this method (line 33) tests to prohibit this Vehicle from exceeding its maximum speed.

The C++ program MyVehicleClassProgram.cpp shown in Figure 10-6 uses the Vehicle class, and the output generated by this program is shown in Figure 10-7.

```
1       // This program uses the programmer-defined Vehicle class.
2       #include "Vehicle.cpp"
3       #include <iostream>
4       using namespace std;
5       int main()
6       {
7           Vehicle vehicleOne;
8
9           vehicleOne.setMaxSpeed(100.0);
10          vehicleOne.setSpeed(35.0);
11          vehicleOne.accelerate(10.0);
12          cout << "The current speed is " << vehicleOne.getSpeed() << endl;
13
14          vehicleOne.accelerate(60.0);
15          cout << "The current speed is " << vehicleOne.getSpeed() << endl;
16
17          return 0;
18      }
```

Figure 10-6 MyVehicleClassProgram that uses the Vehicle class

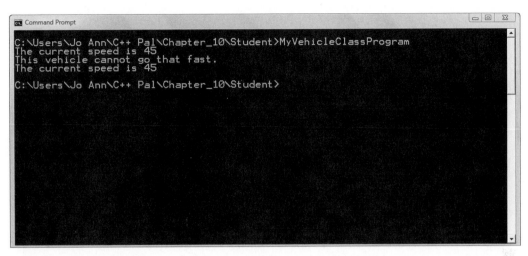

Figure 10-7 Output generated by the MyVehicleClassProgram

Looking at Figure 10-6, you see that line 1 is a comment that describes what the program does. On line 2 you see #include "Vehicle.cpp". This preprocessor directive instructs C++ to include the file that contains the definition of the Vehicle class. Next, on lines 3 and 4, you see the #include directive that allows you to use cout in this program and the using statement you learned about in Chapter 1 of this book. The main function begins on line 5.

On line 7, a Vehicle object is created named vehicleOne. Next, on line 9, the maximum speed for vehicleOne is set to 100.0 miles per hour (mph) using the setMaxSpeed method. Line 10 uses the setSpeed method to set the current speed for vehicleOne at 35.0 mph and on line 11 vehicleOne accelerates by 10.0 mph using the accelerate method. The cout statement on line 12 produces the following output: "The current speed is 45". Notice that the getSpeed method is used in the cout statement to retrieve vehicleOne's current speed. On line 14 vehicleOne invokes the accelerate method again; this time to accelerate by 60.0 mph. Accelerating by 60.0 mph would cause vehicleOne to travel faster than its maximum speed and causes the accelerate method to produce the following output: "This vehicle cannot go that fast". The cout statement on line 15 produces the following output: "The current speed is 45". This output shows that the accelerate method will not allow this Vehicle object to travel faster than its maximum speed.

Now that the Vehicle class is complete, it can be used as a base class. You would like to use the Vehicle class to create a new Automobile class. You realize that an automobile is a vehicle just like the vehicle defined by the Vehicle class. You would like to be able to set a maximum speed, a current speed, and the fuel capacity for the automobile. You would also like to get its maximum speed, its current speed, and its fuel capacity. If you use inheritance, you will able to do all of these actions without having to write any new code. Additionally, you would like to accelerate the automobile; but if you want the automobile to accelerate beyond its maximum speed, you would like to change the message generated to say "This automobile cannot go that fast". You also want to be able to indicate if the automobile has a convertible top. You realize you will have to modify the inherited `accelerate` method and add new data to the `Automobile` class to indicate whether or not a particular `Automobile` object is a convertible, along with get and set methods to set the convertible top status and to get the convertible top status.

Figure 10-8 contains the C++ code that uses inheritance to create a derived class named `Automobile` using the `Vehicle` class as its base class.

```
1       // Automobile.cpp
2       #include "Vehicle.cpp"
3       #include <iostream>
4       using namespace std;
5       class Automobile : public Vehicle
6       {
7          public:
8              void accelerate(double);
9              void setConvertibleStatus(bool);
10             bool getConvertibleStatus();
11         private:
12             bool convertibleStatus;
13      };
14
15      void Automobile::accelerate(double mph)
16      {
17         if(getSpeed() + mph > getMaxSpeed())
18             cout << "This Automobile cannot go that fast" << endl;
19         else
20             setSpeed(getSpeed() + mph);
21      }
22
23      void Automobile::setConvertibleStatus(bool status)
24      {
25         convertibleStatus = status;
26         return;
27      }
28
29      bool Automobile::getConvertibleStatus()
30      {
31         return convertibleStatus;
32      }
```

Figure 10-8 `Automobile` class implemented in C++

Looking at Figure 10-8, you see that line 1 is a comment and on line 2 you see `#include "Vehicle.cpp"`. This preprocessor directive instructs C++ to include the file that contains the definition of the `Vehicle` class. C++ needs to know about the `Vehicle` class in order to create the `Automobile` class. Next, on lines 3 and 4, you see the `#include` directive that allows you to use `cout` in this class's methods and the `using` statement you learned about in Chapter 1 of this book. The `Automobile` class begins on line 5.

As shown on line 5, when you write the declaration for a derived class, you begin with the keyword `class` followed by the name of the derived class (`Automobile`). Next, you include a : (colon) followed by the keyword `public` and then the name of the class from which you are deriving the new class (`Vehicle`).

The keyword `public` specifies a derivation type. A **public** derivation means that all of the `public` members of the base class will be `public` in the derived class. Therefore, you do not have to repeat these members in the derived class; you simply use the inherited members. This means that the new `Automobile` class inherits, and will be able to use, the public methods from the `Vehicle` class. These methods are: `setSpeed`, `getSpeed`, `accelerate`, `setFuelCapacity`, `getFuelCapacity`, `setMaxSpeed`, and `getMaxSpeed`. Now, in the `Automobile` class, you are able to use these `public` methods to gain access to the `private` members (`fuelCapacity`, `maxSpeed`, and `currentSpeed`) in the `Vehicle` class. In the derived `Automobile` class, you can also add new members or modify the inherited members. There are additional derivation types in C++, but in this book, you will always use the `public` derivation type. You will learn more about derivation types when you take additional courses in C++.

On line 12 in Figure 10-8, you see that one `private` data member, `convertibleStatus`, is added to the `Automobile` class. This `bool` data member is used to store a `true` or `false` value and specifies whether or not the `Automobile` has a convertible top. To provide the ability to set a value and get a value for the new `convertibleStatus` data member, two public methods, `setConvertibleStatus` and `getConvertibleStatus`, are added to the `Automobile` class on lines 9 and 10.

On line 8, you see the `accelerate` method. This method has the same signature as the `accelerate` method in the `Vehicle` class.

When you declare a method in a derived class (`Automobile`) with the same signature as a method in the base class (`Vehicle`), the derived class method **overrides** the inherited method. This means the method must be rewritten in the derived class and will be used with `Automobile` objects. The `accelerate` method needs to be rewritten for the `Automobile` class because you want it to generate the message "`This Automobile cannot go that fast`" rather than the message "`This vehicle cannot go that fast.`"

Now, the methods declared in the derived `Automobile` class must be written. The `accelerate` method is written on lines 15 through 21. On line 17, you see the following `if` statement:

```
if(getSpeed() + mph > getMaxSpeed())
```

Notice the test portion of the `if` statement uses the inherited `getSpeed` method to retrieve the value stored in the `private` data member `currentSpeed`, and the inherited `getMaxSpeed` method to retrieve the value stored in the `private` data member `maxSpeed`. You do not have direct access to the `private` members of the base class (`Vehicle`); therefore, the inherited `public` methods must be used to gain access to the `private` data members `currentSpeed` and `maxSpeed`.

On line 18, you see the `cout` statement that generates the modified output: "`This Automobile cannot go that fast`". This statement executes if you try to accelerate the `Automobile`

> **»NOTE**
> In Chapter 7 of this book, you learned that a signature is made up of method (function) name, the number of arguments it receives, and the data type of the arguments.

beyond its maximum speed. If the acceleration does not cause the Automobile to travel at a speed that is beyond its maximum speed, line 20 executes. Line 20 invokes the inherited setSpeed method and passes the acceleration amount (mph) added to the current speed. The current speed is retrieved by using the inherited getSpeed method.

On lines 23 through 27, you see the setConvertibleStatus method, which sets the value of the private bool data member convertibleStatus. And, on lines 29 through 32, you see the getConvertibleStatus method that retrieves the value of the private bool data member convertibleStatus.

USING A DERIVED CLASS IN A C++ PROGRAM

Now that the derived Automobile class is defined, you can use it in a C++ program. The C++ program (MyAutomobileClassProgram.cpp) shown in Figure 10-9 includes a comment on line 1. Line 2 includes the file, Automobile.cpp, that contains the Automobile class definition, line 3 includes <iostream>, and the using statement is on line 4. An Automobile object (automobileOne) is then created on line 7 and a bool variable (convertible) is declared on line 8.

```
1    // This program uses the programmer-defined Automobile class.
2    #include "Automobile.cpp"
3    #include <iostream>
4    using namespace std;
5    int main()
6    {
7        Automobile automobileOne;
8        bool convertible;
9
10       automobileOne.setMaxSpeed(100.0);
11       automobileOne.setSpeed(35.0);
12       automobileOne.accelerate(10.0);
13       cout << "The current speed is " << automobileOne.getSpeed() << endl;
14
15       automobileOne.accelerate(60.0);
16       cout << "The current speed is " << automobileOne.getSpeed() << endl;
17
18       automobileOne.setConvertibleStatus(true);
19       convertible = automobileOne.getConvertibleStatus();
20
21       if(convertible == true)
22          cout << "This automobile is a convertible" << endl;
23       else
24          cout << "This automobile is not a convertible" << endl;
25
26       return 0;
27   }
```

Figure 10-9 MyAutomobileClassProgram that uses the Automobile class

Next, on line 10, the maximum speed for `automobileOne` is set to 100.0 miles per hour (mph) using the inherited `setMaxSpeed` method. Line 11 uses the inherited `setSpeed` method to set the current speed for `automobileOne` at 35.0 mph and on line 12 `automobileOne` accelerates by 10.0 mph using the `accelerate` method that was overridden in the `Automobile` class. The `cout` statement on line 13 produces the following output: "The current speed is 45". Notice that the inherited `getSpeed` method is used in the `cout` statement to retrieve `automobileOne`'s current speed. On line 15, `automobileOne` invokes the overridden `accelerate` method again; this time to accelerate by 60.0 mph. Accelerating by 60.0 mph would cause `automobileOne` to travel faster than its maximum speed, and causes the `accelerate` method that was overridden in the `Automobile` class to produce the following output: "This Automobile cannot go that fast". This output shows that the overridden `accelerate` method is used with an `Automobile` object. The `cout` statement on line 16 produces the following output: "The current speed is 45". This output shows that the `accelerate` method will not allow this `Automobile` object to travel faster than its maximum speed.

Next, on line 18, `automobileOne` invokes the `setConvertibleStatus` method and passes a `true` value that indicates this `Automobile` object is a convertible. The `getConvertibleStatus` method is invoked on line 19 where its return value is assigned to the `bool` variable `convertible`. The value of `convertible` is tested in the `if` statement on line 21. If the value of `convertible` is `true`, the `cout` statement on line 22 executes, generating the following output: "This automobile is a convertible". If the value of `convertible` is `false`, the `cout` statement on line 24 executes, generating the following output: "This automobile is not a convertible".

»NOTE
This chapter has introduced you to the basics of object-oriented programming in C++. You will have to take additional courses in C++ to become a C++ programmer.

The output from the `MyAutomobileClassProgram` is shown in Figure 10-10.

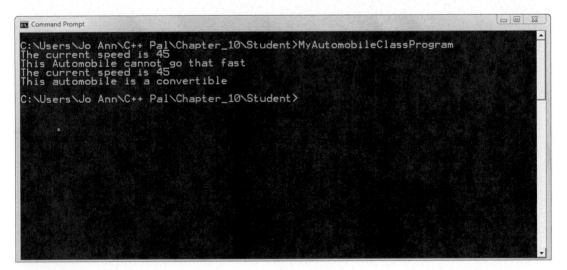

Figure 10-10 `MyAutomobileClassProgram` output

EXERCISE 10-2: USING INHERITANCE TO CREATE A DERIVED CLASS IN C++

In this exercise, you use what you have learned about using inheritance to create a derived class to answer some questions.

1. Which line of code is used to create a derived class named `SubWidget` from a base class named `Widget`?

   a. `class Widget : public SubWidget`

   b. `class SubWidget : base public Widget`

   c. `class Widget : derived public SubWidget`

   d. `class SubWidget : public Widget`

   _____

2. An advantage of using inheritance is:

   a. It maximizes the number of functions.

   b. It allows reuse of code.

   c. It requires no coding.

   _____

3. True or False. The methods in a derived class have direct access to the base class private data members.

   _____

4. True or False. A derived class may add new methods or override existing methods when inheriting from a base class.

   _____

LAB 10-2: USING INHERITANCE TO CREATE A DERIVED CLASS IN C++

In this lab, you create a derived class from a base class and then use the derived class in a C++ program. The program should create two `Motorcycle` objects and then set the `Motorcycle`'s speed, accelerate the `Motorcycle` object, and check its side car status. Use the `Vehicle` and `Automobile` classes that you worked with earlier in this chapter as a guide.

1. Open the file named `Motorcycle.cpp` using Notepad or the text editor of your choice.

2. Create the `Motorcycle` class by deriving it from the `Vehicle` class. Use a `public` derivation.

3. In the `Motorcycle` class, create a private attribute named `sidecar`. The `sidecar` attribute should be data type `bool`.

4. Write a public set method to set the value for `sidecar`.

5. Write a public get method to retrieve the value of `sidecar`.

6. Write a public `accelerate` method. This method overrides the `accelerate` method inherited from the `Vehicle` class. Change the message in the `accelerate` method so the following is displayed when the `Motorcycle` tries to accelerate beyond its maximum speed: "`This Motorcycle cannot go that fast`".

7. Save this class file, `Motorcycle.cpp`, in a directory of your choice and then open the file named `MyMotorcycleClassProgram.cpp`.

8. In the `MyMotorcycleClassProgram`, create two `Motorcycle` objects named `motorCycleOne` and `motorCycleTwo`.

9. Set the `sidecar` value of `motorcycleOne` to `true` and the `sidecar` value of `motorcycleTwo` to `false`.

10. Set `motorcycleOne`'s maximum speed to 90 and `motorcycleTwo`'s maximum speed to 85.

11. Set `motorcycleOne`'s current speed to 65 and `motorcycleTwo`'s current speed to 60.

12. Accelerate `motorcycleOne` by 30 miles per hour (mph) and accelerate `motorcycleTwo` by 20 mph.

13. Print the current speed of `motorcycleOne` and `motorcycleTwo`.

14. Determine if `motorcycleOne` and `motorcycleTwo` have side cars. If yes, display the following: "This motorcycle has a side car". If not, display the following: "`This motorcycle does not have a side car`".

15. Save `MyMotorcycleClassProgram.cpp` in the same directory as `Motorcycle.cpp`.

16. Compile the source code file `MyMotorCycleClassProgram.cpp`.

17. Execute the program.

18. Record the output below.

_____

_____

_____

_____

_____

INDEX